IT'S NOT ABOUT FOOD

Change Your Mind; Change Your Life; End Your Obsession with Food and Weight

CAROL EMERY NORMANDI AND

LAURELEE ROARK

A PERIGEE BOOK

A Perigee Book
Published by The Berkley Publishing Group
A division of Penguin Putnam Inc.
375 Hudson Street
New York, New York 10014

Book design by Chris Welch

Published simultaneously in Canada.

Grosset/Putnam edition: May 1998
First Perigee edition: May 1999
Perigee ISBN: 0-399-52502-5

The Penguin Putnam Inc. World Wide Web site address is
http://www.penguinputnam.com

The Library of Congress has catalogued the
Grosset/Putnam edition as follows:

Normandi, Carol Emery.
It's not about food / by Carol Emery Normandi and Laurelee Roark.
p. cm.
Includes index.
ISBN 0-399-14330-0
1. Eating disorders—Popular works. 2. Eating disorders—
Psychological aspects. 3. Obsessive-compulsive disorders—
Popular works. I. Roark, Laurelee. II. Title.
RC552.E18N67 1998
616.85'26—dc21 97-36328 CIP

Printed in the United States of America

10 9 8 7 6 5 4 3 2 1

PUBLISHER'S NOTE
Every effort has been made to ensure that the information contained in this book is complete and accurate. However, neither the publisher nor the author is engaged in rendering professional advice or services to the individual reader. The ideas, procedures, and suggestions contained in this book are not intended as a substitute for consulting with your physician. All matters regarding your health require medical supervision. Neither the author nor the publisher shall be liable or responsible for any loss or damage allegedly arising from any information or suggestion in this book.

LAURELEE'S ACKNOWLEDGMENTS

I wish to acknowledge the friends and family that I've had the honor and privilege to have around me as I went through the process of my recovery from my eating disorder and the writing of this book.

The first is my business and book partner, my best girlfriend, Carol Normandi. How anyone writes a book by themselves, I do not know. I could not have done it without you.

Also, my best boyfriend, my husband, James O'Dell. He thinks I'm great, believes in me, and supports all my various projects one hundred percent. Plus, he has a very sweet heart.

My wonderful son, Clinton Ragsdale. He never ceases to amaze me with his humor, truth, and through-and-through goodness.

My mother, Edith Brehm, who continues to challenge me as we both go through the twists and turns of her life.

My sisters and brothers, Keith, Melanie, Trisha, Kathy, and Jimmy, who show me unconditional love and support no matter how crazy this Californian may get.

My dear friend, Kenneth Horner, who was with me as I went through the last year of my eating disorder and the even more insane time of my early recovery; his faith and love held me together through many a dark night of the soul.

Linda Johnson, the first person to "get" what I was trying to do, and together with me, set up the first Beyond Hunger group. I will be eternally grateful for her foresight.

To the many people who helped me through my various recoveries; my therapists, my twelve-step sponsors, and my loving "chosen family." I am honored to know you and to let you get to know me.

My salon clients and fellow hairdressers who have put up with me as I have gone through the transitions of trying to balance my different jobs. Thanks for putting up with me when stuff fell through the cracks.

For many others too numerous to mention here, I love you back, *namaste.*

CAROL'S ACKNOWLEDGMENTS

With love and gratitude, I thank my parents, Charles and Doreen Emery, for the love and nurturance they gave me (and continue to give), which laid the foundation for my life and my recovery. This is the greatest gift of all.

I thank my husband, Jim Normandi, for his love, humor, commitment, passion, truth, and excellent fathering, which have made my life full and precious. Thank you for teaching me to love myself exactly as I am, for believing in and supporting this project, and for tending the hearth and the babies, no matter how stressful.

I thank my sister, Charlotte Emery Lindborg, for literally saving my life by sharing her own recovery with me, and for always being there with love, presence, and wisdom no matter where I am.

I thank my dear friend and partner, Laurelee Roark, for her compassion and passion that birthed Beyond Hunger, and for her endless commitment, time, and energy that keep Beyond Hunger alive. Thank you for "dreaming" the book and for keeping the dream and our relationship alive with your loving humor, persistence, and patience.

I thank my whole family for the many ways they've supported me during my recovery and the creation of this book: Burr Emery (for believing in me), and his family, Elaine, Danielle, and Kyle; Karl, Dillon, Beau, and Torgeir Lindborg (especially Dillon and Beauie for walking—or not walking—that extra mile); Jim and Winnie

Normandi for their generous, unconditional love and support; Angela, Doug, Alanna, and Maria DeSalvo for helping me survive these last few years; and Tony Normandi and Nana Kay Anderson.

I thank my friend, Wendy Young Howard, for her friendship, commitment, integrity, and intuition that in many ways supported me in creating this book. I thank Debbie Epidendio and Lisa Hoye for that precious day when they watched my kids while I wrote. I thank all of my friends who have given me their guidance and kept me sane during this process, providing me with a richness of life that I will always be grateful for.

I am grateful for all of the people who helped in my recovery to find my true self: Jay Rice, Nora Riley, Molly Brown, and The Center for Attitudinal Healing. I thank all of my clients, who in their bravery and wisdom have taught me about the miracles of love and healing.

And last but not least, I thank my children, Traver and Maya, who have brought to me the greatest challenges and the greatest joys in remembering the magic of brilliant spirits in exquisite bodies.

CAROL AND LAURELEE'S ACKNOWLEDGMENTS

Support for the creation of Beyond Hunger and the subsequent writing of this book came from many different sources and in many different ways.

We would first like to thank the women whose experiences, courage, and dreams are the stories that form the basis of the book. Without these women who opened themselves up, spoke their truth, and allowed us to witness their process, we would not have been able to be present for the wondrous and remarkable miracles of recovery.

There were many different angels from the very start. The first is

Patti Breitman, the best book agent in the world. Throughout this incredible process we have always felt her belief in us, her emotional, spiritual, and practical support, her inspiration and her persistent nudging.

We had different "coaches" or editors who made sense of our words so that the book would be readable (we knew what we were saying even if no one else did). We thank Kate Fitzsimmons and Melba Beals, who helped us clarify what we wanted to say and how we wanted to say it. But it was Hal Bennet, the amazing "Book Doctor," who helped us find our voice and our vision. He held our hands, told us that we were doing great while marking up our chapters with red and sometimes green ink, and in the end made it possible for us to get the book out there in our own words while making sure it was in English.

We are deeply indebted to the people behind the scenes of Beyond Hunger; the Beyond Hunger therapists, Elizabeth Scott and Sue Lilledahl; our board members, past and present, including Jill DeBow, Doug DeSalvo, Cindy Dooling, Hilary King Flye, Linda Luchessa, Roxanne Peterson, Annie Rohrbach, Nan Stockhom, Patty Ward, and Wendy Young; Vajra Farnsworth, who for years volunteered not only her time and resources but also her heart and her enthusiastic support; and our volunteer angels, Paula Capocchi and Maria Dorio. We thank Ken Horner for the never-ending many ways in which he kept Beyond Hunger alive. We thank Charles and Doreen Emery for their endless hours of volunteer babysitting so that we could write this book. We thank Charlotte Emery Lindborg for her skillful word processing, her feminine insight that helped us stay on track, and her artistic talent that created our gorgeous goddesses. We thank all of the people at the Marin Healing Arts Center for providing a loving creative and spiritual home for our work. Thanks to all of the people who have not only given freely their time, their ideas, and their money, but most of all their love and support to us in thousands of different ways. We could not have done this work without you.

We thank Jane Hirschmann and Carol Munter for your inspirational and groundbreaking work. We are touched by the eloquence of your foreword and by your willingness to share your support and expertise with us and Beyond Hunger.

We are very grateful to Sheila Curry, our excellent editor, who really picked up the ball that was thrown to her and carried us through to completion with style, humor, and levelheadedness. We are also grateful to Jane Isay and Putnam Publishing for believing in the book in the first place.

Lastly, we would like to thank our true angel, Joy Silver Johnston, who died before our book was completed. As our book's midwife, she believed in us, understood us, and held the dream with us. Her love, support, and wisdom still inspire us.

To all of the women, men, and children who died from eating disorders before discovering the true sacredness of their bodies and their Selves

CONTENTS

INTRODUCTION

In the beginning of each of our twelve-week Beyond Hunger support groups we run for individuals with eating disorders, we are always moved by the members' stories of what they have been through. It reminds us of the strength, tenacity, and courage that we all carry within us to survive and carry on even in the most painful circumstances. We came to this work because the work came through us. We do this work because it feeds our souls. As the groups continue we are touched by the unique beauty of each participant as they come alive and reveal themselves to each other. We learn to expand our own perception of beauty when we start to see their inner beauty unfold. As the group members show their compassion and support for each other we are reminded of the healing power of love. As they learn to look within and find their own wisdom and truth we are continually amazed that the wisdom is always lying right beneath the surface, just waiting to be seen. We get to witness the birth of creativity, passion, and power. And when our members begin to get a glimpse of who they really are, above and beyond the fat on their bellies, we get to witness a spiritual awakening—which awakens our own spirits.

We started Beyond Hunger because we had both struggled with eating disorders for many years and discovered in our own recovery that most of the programs available did not give us what we needed. We found that to achieve true, permanent recovery we had to address the physical, emotional, and spiritual wounds that lay at the core of our eating disorders. We named our groups Beyond Hunger because we felt that in order to recover from eating disorders, we needed to go beyond the hunger of our physical bodies and meet the hunger that resides in our very souls. We had to look deep into ourselves to find out what drives us to obsessive eating, body loathing, and self-hatred. We developed a program using what had worked for us personally and for the women who were in the first few groups. Beyond Hunger, Inc., evolved to the point that in the early '90s we became a nonprofit organization in order to continue our groups and workshops and to educate the general public about eating disorders. Our groups and workshops are held in northern California.

Doing this work means we also get to be a part of a national movement to stop dieting, stop obsessing about food and weight, stop objectifying and hating our bodies, and start living our lives, treating ourselves and each other with love and respect. We will never be free from oppression until we can take ourselves out of the bondage of self-hatred and then reclaim our bodies and our wisdom as sacred. Even amidst the increasing numbers of eating disorders and body-image disturbances among our youth, it is heartening to know that there is a growing movement of people in this country who are committed to stopping this trend. We are eternally grateful to the pioneers before us who had the courage, wisdom, and perseverance to speak their truth to the world. They have not only had a profound impact on our own recovery but have also paved the way for our voices to be heard and for our book to be written.

It's Not about Food is not another diet book, a lose-ten-pounds-while-you-sleep or what-you-should-and-should-not-eat book. It's a book about going beneath the symptoms of the eating disorder, finding and embracing the emotional, physical, and spiritual wounds that are at the core of the eating disorder, and healing them. It's *not* about dieting. It's about freedom from the diet/binge cycle, starvation, and body hatred. It's *not* about being thin. It's about rebelling against the cultural expectations to have a "perfect" body and learning to embrace the sacred feminine within us. It's *not* about a quick fix. It's about transformation and finding a true long-lasting recovery. It's about reclaiming your life.

By reading *It's Not about Food* you will discover the differences between your physical hunger and emotional hunger. You will develop compassion for your self and your eating disorder, transforming whatever shame and hatred you have into a deep respect for your eating disorder's ability to keep you alive and be the voice for your soul. You will understand the underlying emotional reasons for your eating disorder and learn to take care of yourself in ways other than overeating, undereating, or obsessing about food and weight. You will discover a new and loving relationship with your body, honoring it no matter what size, shape, or age. You will explore how to set boundaries, say no, and nurture yourself in ways that feed your soul. You will deepen your connection with your own spiritual self and listen to your inner voice that can guide you to live in your own truth and create your own dreams.

What we say in this book may make you scared, mad, happy, or provoke any number of other reactions. You may actually feel quite relieved or validated for what your struggle has been about. We suggest you read this book using your own internal guidance. Take every example, suggestion, and exercise and ask yourself if it applies to you. Give yourself permission to sort out what is true for you and what isn't. Remember, much of what is in this book comes from our experience and perspective. You may agree with all of it, some of it, or none of it. As the old twelve-step saying goes, "Just take what you need and leave the rest."

Both of our stories are interwoven throughout this book. We also use stories of women who have gone through the program. These quotes are composites of many of the women we've worked with through the years and have been slightly altered in order to protect their anonymity. Some of these stories may ring true for you and others may not. Remember, everyone's experience is different.

We have written this book about women and for women because we wanted to write it from our own experience. In addition, part of the source of body image and eating disorders has been the cultural oppression of women. We are very aware that eating disorders are increasing among men. They too suffer from cultural pressures to have a certain body type, behave a certain way, and play a certain role in our society. We also acknowledge that this book has been written from the perspective of two American heterosexual white women and we have not addressed different issues that might arise for people of different color, economic status, sexual preference, religious beliefs, or ethnic background. However, what we have experienced in our groups is that although many of the causes and symptoms of the eating disorders are different for different people, the healing message is always the same: We are all sacred, to be honored and respected for our uniqueness.

We know that it is possible to live without constantly obsessing about bodies and food, and without self-hatred and shame. We know there is an abundance of creativity, passion, and power within all of us that is just waiting to be discovered. And we've found that listening to our eating disorders is the pathway to discovery. How we walk down this pathway is different for everyone. This is a book about our journeys as well as those of the many women whom we have worked with over the years. We hope that you will be loving with yourself as you join us on the journey beyond hunger.

FOREWORD

We are approaching the twenty-first century. Everyone agrees that in the past few decades, women have made enormous gains—politically, economically, and psychologically. Yet millions of women still wake up each morning, look in the mirror, and say, "Yuck."

Sadly, we live in a culture in which body hatred and food preoccupation are considered normal components of feminine development and a completely unrealistic ideal of thinness holds sway. Study after study proves the ineffectiveness of dieting, yet each new weight-reduction scheme is embraced wholeheartedly by the female population. Reports of possible fatal side effects of new weight-loss medications provoke dismay about the loss of the magic bullet rather than despair about possible damage already done.

It is true that the pressure to diet and bodyshape is enormous. But given decades of failed attempts to change our basic shapes, why do we women continue to buy in? Why do we cling to the notion that there is such a thing as a perfect thigh? Just who made that determination? And why are we so quick to assume that our stomachs should be flat when for centuries our rounded bellies symbolized the essence of female richness and fecundity?

Indeed, women's lives have changed dramatically. But women's continuing progress in the direction of equality has induced a strong backlash, some of which takes the form of increased pressure to diet and bodyshape. In our view, women succumb to this pressure because centuries of inequality have taken their toll. Discriminated against in subtle and not so subtle ways, millions of us have internalized the sense that we are "less than" and certainly not good enough the way we are. Even today, despite our impressive strides in the world—more women in elected positions, more economic clout, more access to education and jobs—women are still struggling for the basic rights of economic parity, safety at home and on the streets, reproductive freedom, and affordable child care. Body hatred and chronic dieting prove that at the level of our deepest feelings, we women are still in a lot of trouble. In other words, progress aside, we still feel bad about ourselves.

When a woman—whatever her size or shape—says, "I feel fat," she is speaking in a code only women understand. When a woman says, "I feel fat," in the guise of criticizing her body, she is actually condemning herself for a whole range of thoughts and feelings that pertain to how much space she feels permitted to occupy in the world.

Each time a woman says, "I feel fat," she is doing what she has been taught to do: she is making a comment about her body instead of sorting through the conflicting feelings or thoughts that are disturbing her at that moment. The chances are that after making the detour to her body, she will then have the fantasy that if she would just lose weight or somehow transform the contours of her body, everything about her and her world would be just fine. But losing weight never solves the problem. The problems that cause women to focus on what they eat and what they weigh require much thought, considerable attention, and lots of compassion. Many of women's conflicting thoughts and feelings are rooted in the dilemma of being female in a culture that feels ambivalent about women's participation.

Mostly, women don't speak directly about their shaky sense of entitlement. Instead, raised as girls, they speak endlessly about their bodies and their need to transform them rather than the world.

Carol Normandi and Laurelee Roark understand that *It's Not about Food*, that women suffering from eating problems are living lives filled with detours. In others words, eating problems and body image problems are really feeling problems in disguise. In moving personal accounts of their own and their clients' struggles to work through the problems that underlie their preoccupation with food and weight, they offer testimony to the possibility of curing eating problems. Through numerous creative exercises, Normandi and Roark give readers the tools with which to end this debilitating preoccupation with what we eat and what we weigh. They urge women to take up as much space as they need; to stop the dieting that has become a lifelong, life-draining preoccupation; to learn to eat in response to physiological hunger and to get in touch with those feelings that send them to food in the first place. Women who read this book will be inspired to throw away their diets and scales and pick up on the nurturing, caring voice presented in these pages.

The time has come for us women to enjoy our bodies in all their diversity, to reclaim our appetites, our bodies, and our lives. Imagine what would happen if all the women in the world stopped using body preoccupation and dieting to keep themselves confined! Normandi and Roark's book is part of that struggle, an important and necessary voice in our ever-growing anti-diet movement.

Jane R. Hirschmann and Carol H. Munter,
authors of *Overcoming Overeating* and
When Women Stop Hating Their Bodies

Chapter 1

WHAT'S IT REALLY ABOUT? LIFE BEYOND HUNGER

There was a time when you were not a slave, remember that. You walked alone, full of laughter, you bathed bare bellied. You say you have lost all recollection of it, remember! You say there are not words to describe it; you say it does not exist. But remember! Make an effort to remember! or failing that, invent.

—MONIQUE WITTIG, *Les Guerillères*

I have been a compulsive eater ever since high school, when I became aware of messages that made me feel my body was not acceptable the way it was. I was a teenage model in the sixties. When Twiggy came on the fashion scene, we were all urged to weigh less than one hundred pounds. At a time when my body was still developing calcium for my bones and teeth, hormones for my reproductive system, and cells for my brain, I was eating less than a thousand calories a day. I came to believe that if I would just lose a few pounds my body and my self would then be accepted. Somehow, because I didn't have the "perfect" body, I got the message that my whole being was defective. Instead of having a problem—a defective body—I became the problem—a defective person.

I would have tried anything to get thin and stay thin. I believed that if I could be thin, then I could be happy, joyous, and free. When I was fat and bingeing, I was convinced I would be happy if I was thin and dieting. When I was thin and dieting I was terrified that soon I would be fat and bingeing again. Years of my life went by in this pattern, some of them only highlighted by what I weighed or what diet I was on. My level of self-hatred and despair was unbearable. I thought all that was wrong with me could be measured by pounds. Thinness was my god and I was on a spiritual quest. I sought refuge from pain in the churches of Weight Watchers, Jenny Craig, and Dr. Atkins diets. I was looking outside myself to fix the ache inside me.

—Laurelee

Millions of American women will find the above story familiar. The struggle with dieting, loathing our bodies, and looking outside ourselves to feel better has become an integral part of so many of our daily lives. To get through a day without worrying about what to eat, how it will make us fat, or what our body looks like, is a difficult challenge for many women and men. Thinness through dieting has become our cultural obsession and for many has evolved into a reason for being.

Even though 98 percent of all dieters regain their weight back within five years, and 95 percent within two years, Americans continue to be obsessed with dieting. In 1990 it was estimated that the weight-loss business made $32 billion in 1989 and was expected to exceed $50 billion by 1995 (*US News & World Report*, 1990). Pick a day and you'll find more than one fourth of American women on a diet, with as many as half of them "cheating," completing, or beginning a diet cycle all over again (Roberta Seid, *Never Too Thin*).

As Americans are spending their valuable time and resources on finding the perfect body through dieting, they are actually placing themselves at risk of developing an eating disorder. Research indicates that self-imposed dieting can result in eating binges and in preoccupation with food and eating (Polivy, *Journal of the American Dietetic Association*, 1996) and that individuals who diet are eight times more likely to develop eating disorders (L. K. George Hsu, *Eating Disorders*).

Many women have no idea how insidious their eating disorders will become when they start dieting and starving themselves. They then often yo-yo up and down the scale. Their life becomes consumed by their weight and the desire to stay ultrathin. They have become addicted to dieting and have no idea what their natural weight is.

I started dieting when I was thirteen. As I look back now, I can see that I had feelings of insecurity that were surfacing as I struggled with relationships, my identity, and my sexuality. Back then it just felt like I was too fat. As my body began to change from a normal, undeveloped child to a rounder, curvier woman, I held on to the ideals I saw in the media of the very thin, tall, hard bodies that defined beauty. My body was wrong. All my emotional struggles and insecurities became placed on my body. The first day I put myself on a diet, I stopped listening to the wisdom and truth of my own body. I began instead the pattern of forcing myself to conform to cultural standards that were impossible for me to obtain. My soul was crying out for love, for reassurance, security, and emotional soothing during a very overwhelming, confusing period in my life. The only way I knew how to soothe myself was to eat. The only way I knew how to be accepted was to diet. My voice, my cry for help became buried under the obsession and compulsion of dieting and bingeing, bingeing and purging.

—Carol

Eating disorders start early and for those afflicted it doesn't stop easily. According to the National Association of Anorexia Nervosa and Associated Disorders (ANAD), 86 percent of victims of eating disorders report the onset of their illness by age twenty, with 33 percent reporting onset between the ages of eleven to fifteen. The way our youth have incorporated this obsession with food and weight into the development of self-esteem is frightening. In a survey done by Mellin, Irwin, and Scully (1982), 65 percent of eleven-year-old girls worry that they are too fat, and approximately 80 percent of eleven-year-old girls reported dieting behaviors. It is also estimated that 90 percent of high school junior and senior adolescents diet regularly. The Council on Size and Weight Discrimination reports that young girls are more afraid of becoming fat than they are of nuclear war, cancer, or losing their parents.

The enormity of the problem cannot be fully understood until we acknowledge it in terms of lost and wasted lives. According to the American Anorexia/Bulimia Association, one out of every one hundred teenage girls becomes anorexic, and 10 percent of them may die as a result. Over a thousand women die every year of anorexia. This figure does not include bulimics or compulsive eaters who die as a result of their eating disorder.

Of all of the eating-disorder patients, 90 percent are female. To be a woman in our culture is to be on a diet, worried about weight, or on the verge of an eating disorder. To be a woman is to hate our bodies and to strive for an ideal body that is unattainable and unnatural for most of us. Fashion models, who embody the ideal of feminine beauty, weigh about 23 percent less than the national average woman. We now have the youngest, skinniest, and most anorexic models that we have had for twenty years. Every month, in any beauty magazine, one can see mere children, or at least childlike bodies, selling clothes being pitched to much more mature women.

How can we continue to ignore the devastating impact our culture is having on our women and girls? A recent study showed that social comparison and societal factors were significant predictors of body dissatisfaction and eating disturbance (*International Journal of Eating Disorders,* March 1996). Another study showed that the amount of time watching soaps and movies encouraged body dissatisfaction, and the watching of music videos led to a drive for thinness (*International Journal of Eating Disorders,* September, 1996).

In a 1984 *Glamour* magazine survey of 33,000 women by Drs. Wayne and Susan Wooley of the University of Cincinnati College of Medicine, 75 percent of eighteen- to thirty-five-year-old American women felt "fat," but only 25 percent of them were defined as medically overweight. In a culture in which the feminine is devalued, most women are ashamed of those parts of the body that contribute to the female shape—their stomachs, hips, thighs, and breasts. The shame is strong enough to drive them to "improve" their appearance by cosmetic surgery. In fact, it's estimated that 250,000 liposuctions are performed every year in the United States. The very young age that most girls are pressured to start seriously dieting—adolescence—is when their bodies turn decidedly feminine, suddenly departing, quite naturally, from the ideal that most models represent. So many adolescent girls find that their ideal body shape is the shape of a boy: flat, toned stomach, concave chest, and slim hips.

All my life I heard, "you have such a pretty face." That statement almost killed me. I would have done anything to lose weight and I did do lots of crazy things. I started taking diet pills (speed) in order to lose weight. I became bulimic and threw up after every meal to lose weight. I have taken laxatives and had colonics. I had urine shots from a doctor and was put on a fast by a medical group. Nothing worked for very long. I always returned to my normal size. Big. But recently I went back to visit my family in Europe and met with my women cousins and aunts. I saw my own body type and realized that I had been trying to be a size that just wasn't natural for my heritage.

—Julie

In America we have racism, ageism, sexism, and sizism. Though it is not very acceptable to call people ethnic names or to refer to someone as old, nothing stops the media, the friends, or the families from commenting on someone's weight. Names are called, jobs are lost, marriages break up, and everyone "understands," particularly if the person is "too fat." An overweight woman walking down the street has no defense against the looks and the raised eyebrows. This levies a heavy toll on these women. Julie's story is an example of a woman whose genetic heritage determined her body size. Yet we have no room for such individualized characteristics in our society. Even genetically large women may try to force their bodies to conform to the arbitrary ideals of society. Even if they are not "overweight" according to their genetic heritage, they are *judged* to be; many times women gain weight in order to protect themselves from the attacks. It can become a vicious cycle. The same weight is gained and lost hundreds of time. Not only does the person's weight wildly fluctuate but with each diet their total body weight may very well be inching up.

Women in this culture have an enormous pressure on them to be perfect. This pressure is put on them early on and is maintained until the day they die. Somewhere along the line many internalize the pressure. The pressure builds and builds, until it is overwhelming, even for the strongest of the strong, the brightest of the bright, and the prettiest of the pretty. Like a cancer that stalks the cells, the push to be sexier, younger, thinner, smarter, nicer, and more successful than everybody else, eats away at a woman's soul. Finally her self-esteem, her self-will, and her self-control are gone, and soon she has no self at all. The expectation to be superwoman and superthin is undermining a whole generation of women. Dieting and obsessing about food, weight, and body image represent the *norm* for girls and women, not the *exception*.

However shocking it may be, we believe that the women who develop a full-blown eating disorder and who choose recovery are the luckiest of all. They can heal. They can have hope and a chance of peace within. Unfortunately not all women recover. Those who die of eating disorders have paid the highest price of all for living as females in a society that relentlessly dictated that there was only one way to be as a woman. Women's evolution at this time is demanding that we go beneath the obsession about counting calories and losing weight, and reclaim our sacredness as women, our right to our own voices and our ability to make our own choices. Until we can do this with the most fundamental issue of food and body, we will be forever stuck in an obsession that keeps us from our true selves.

Many women we have worked with at Beyond Hunger have very specific reasons for first starting to diet or eat compulsively. Some are simple. Others are so complex that it takes the woman years to sort through all the twists and turns and to find the source of her disorder. Often it is a matter of not having the support of the culture to become a mature woman whose experiences are acknowledged and validated by herself—a woman who can draw on her own internal resources to cope with life's challenges. Our society tells us that what matters is how we look. If we look like the ideal woman, then we must be that woman. If we don't look the part then we aren't.

Intense pressure to conform to cultural ideals is experienced by young girls. Many of them start taking pills, drinking, and smoking in order to control their weight. Others start these behaviors in order to ignore or eradicate feelings or as a reaction to what they must do to cope with growing up female in this culture, where their bodies are up for review every day of their lives.

It is a whole lot easier to believe that the problem is with them, rather than with the culture. It is easier to attack the victim than to try to change the perpetrator, especially when the perpetrator is society. Women who struggle with eating disorders are battling not only their own personal demons but also the demons of their culture. Just as we were taught to tie our shoes and taught to drive a car, we were taught to hate our bodies, our appetites, our needs, and ourselves. We have not been taught to be powerful, rational adults, but instead to be sexy little girls. We have learned how to get along in this culture by following the advice of beauty magazines, diet centers, and other women who are getting face lifts and tummy tucks rather than honoring their age. We have taken the battles raged against women and turned the war against ourselves. Some women respond by staying as numb as possible, with overeating or undereating, alcohol, and drugs. Some live in dark rooms in the despair of depression, and some kill themselves. Whatever method they use, they are trying to stop the pain of living in a culture that doesn't support them, doesn't understand them, and doesn't honor the feminine.

Eating disorders aren't about food, which is why diets don't work. We have seen over and over that once the reasons for over- or undereating have been understood, processed, and then let go, the behavior stops and the woman's body returns to her natural body size. No dieting, no shots, no weight reduction pills, no deprivation of any kind is necessary. If we stay focused on the symptoms we don't hear the message we are trying to tell ourselves. The very problem that we are trying to get rid of is actually trying to tell us something. When we can finally listen, then our so-called enemies of fat and food can turn into allies. Food and fat are not killing us, the obsession to control them is.

> *When I was twelve, my sister got married. It was a huge affair. My part in the wedding was to be one of the bridesmaids. All of her other bridesmaids were older than me, pretty and thin. I was a chubby adolescent with pimples and braces. My mother and sister wanted me to go on a five-hundred-calorie-a-day diet for two months before the wedding. The only way I would do it was if they promised to give me a five-pound bar of Hershey's chocolate the day after the wedding. I lost thirty pounds and everyone said I looked great. But all I could think of was the chocolate I would get the next day. I put the weight back on, plus more, immediately. This was the first of many times I would "yo-yo diet," a practice that left me weighing more than three hundred pounds before I was thirty.*
>
> —*Maggie*

When we hear over and over again that we should be dieting and forcing our bodies to meet an unrealistic standard, we begin to believe that we are at fault. We believe we are weak willed because we are not thin, and failures because we can't keep to the strict deprivation diets we have been told we must follow. Although the prevention and treatment of eating disorders is beginning to change, incorporating the cultural and psychological components, many of us have already had years of experience being misunderstood, mislabeled, and mistreated.

We believe that all of us who struggle with weight and food issues, whether it be anorexia, bulimia, or compulsive overeating (defined as binge eating disorder in the *Diagnostic and Statistical Manual of Mental Disorders IV*), are strong, sensitive women who are mirroring these cultural wounds back to society and sending the message through our bodies that we cannot and will not take it anymore.

Only by allowing ourselves to go beneath the symptoms, to understand the underlying feelings and the internal struggles within ourselves, can we hear this message ourselves and reach true recovery and freedom for our bodies, our selves, and our culture. In undertaking this challenge we are bringing to consciousness the emergence of the true feminine.

In our groups we combine women with all eating disorders together because we believe that although women manifest the symptoms differently, the core issue is still the same: learning to love and respect ourselves and our uniqueness. They also learn from each other. The compulsive eater who is often large can see the struggle of the anorexic, who is never thin enough. The anorexic, by watching the compulsive eater, can see the struggle of accepting her body no matter what size it is. The bulimic, who usually begins as a compulsive eater and then controls her weight by purging, learns from both the compulsive eater and the anorexic. Some women have experienced all three of these disorders at some point in time. The three eating disorders are so complex and interrelated that it's difficult to separate them.

Sometimes women with a particular eating disorder will alienate themselves from another eating disorder by judging it, thinking "Well, at least I don't throw up," or "If I was as thin as you I wouldn't be complaining," or "I may be starving myself but at least I'm not fat." This behavior is understandable because we as women have learned to be critical of ourselves and each other and have received the message that eating disorders are shameful. But we strongly believe that although each eating disorder has different symptoms and treatment needs, by rigidly separating them and judging one or another as better or worse we are again dividing and conquering ourselves as women. Whether you are in the hospital fighting for your life because you are emaciated, trying to keep from throwing up in the toilet for the hundredth time, or fighting to stop the dieting cycle and honor a body that has been the subject of shame and ridicule for your whole life, you are trying to cope with what it means to be a woman in today's world. And together, as men and women, we must stand united in finding a healthier way to live in our bodies, minds, and souls so that our children can live a life feeling proud of who they are no matter what shape or size.

There are many books written that define these three eating disorders and explore in depth the physical, psychological, and cultural causes and treatment of eating disorders. We are not attempting to do the same. We know what it's like to read a book written by an "expert" in the field that describes our behaviors and all the reasons why we're doing these things. Sometimes it can feel like being a monkey in a cage, with some outside observer studying and theorizing about us, but not really connecting with us as spiritual beings. Although we define the three eating disorders briefly, our main goal in this book is to support you in going within yourself and listening to the voice of your eating disorder, to find your own unique reasons for developing an eating disorder, and to help you discover what it is that you need to heal. In our experiences we have found that although many books were helpful, the most powerful work for us was going within ourselves, sometimes with the help of a caring therapist, support group, or a good friend, to find the way out.

When I came home from my doctor's appointment I was upset. I didn't know just how upset I was until much later. The doctor had told me for the hundredth time to lose some weight. My cholesterol was up, my blood pressure was dangerously high, and I had back pains all day long.

These things worried me and as I sat in the doctor's office I heard myself promising to go on a restrictive diet the very next day. Armed with a book on fat grams, a six-pack of liquid drink mix and some high-fiber bars, I left the doctor's office feeling much better. I was confident that I was back on the road to health and that I would have a much thinner body in just six weeks.

However, by the time I got home I was feeling nervous at the thought of a month on the new diet plan. I calmed myself down by telling myself that I could eat anything I wanted tonight because after tonight I would never be "bad" again.

By six o'clock I had eaten my dinner. By six-thirty I had eaten a pint of ice cream. By seven o'clock I had made a bowl of popcorn to eat while watching TV. By seven-forty-five I had eaten the popcorn and was starting on the bag of potato chips that I hid from myself in a cabinet above the stove. By eight-thirty I finished the potato chips and had eaten my next day's supply of high-fiber bars. Now I was into some of my liquid diet drinks. By nine-fifteen I was thawing out a frozen cake that was in the freezer. I continued eating throughout the night until twelve o'clock, when I was passed out on the couch in front of the TV, with a raging headache and very painful stomachache. However, the panic I had felt all night long was gone at last.

—Lisa

Lisa was mostly unconscious about what she was doing throughout this whole episode. She only knew that she had to eat, and had to keep on eating until the panic stopped. She had eaten this way many times before and she always felt that she would go on that diet Monday, or on the first of the month, or at least by six weeks before she had to see her doctor again.

Lisa's compulsive eating went on for a very long time and Lisa got more and more depressed and sad, and she put on more and more weight. Her whole world became only what she could or could not eat, how big she was, or how much weight she would lose if she could just stick to a diet. She never got to know what was truly bothering her or making her unhappy. She didn't know why she was depressed; she only knew she was fat. She didn't know why she was sad; she only knew she had no willpower. She didn't know why she was panicky; she only knew that her life was unbearable.

She had no idea that the real problem was not her eating but the way she was trying to take care of herself. She also didn't know that dieting was actually making her eating disorder worse, and that the cure was not fat-gram information, not liquid diet drinks, not high-fiber bars—not controlling her food whatsoever!

Like Lisa, the compulsive eater eats not only when she is physically hungry, but also when she is emotionally hungry. For the compulsive eater who is a chronic dieter, it's important to stop all diets, to legalize food and let herself eat, becoming her own diet expert and trusting her own body wisdom. This helps the compulsive eater step out of the diet/binge cycle and into her body, relearning the natural cues of physical hunger and fullness. At the same time the compulsive eater can learn how to identify emotional hunger and nurture herself in ways other than food, allowing herself to experience her own feelings without overeating. The compulsive eater also usually feels shame and hatred for her body, but she can work toward loving and accepting her body no matter how different it is from the cultural ideal.

> *My girlfriends and I started a diet when we were fifteen years old and were taking gymnastics. We all lost weight, got a lot of attention, and looked good in our leotards. My coach, my peers, and my parents were proud of my athletic abilities and my "look." But, I wanted to get even thinner than that. So I did. I got thinner and thinner until finally the summer of my seventeenth birthday, my parents put me in the hospital. I was force fed and had to go to therapy sessions three times a day. I couldn't stand the weight my body was putting on but I wanted to get out of the hospital as soon as I could. So I gained twenty pounds and they let me go. I felt like I couldn't compete at this "gross weight." I went on another diet and within three months I was down to eighty-five pounds. Again. When I was around my parents, I wore very baggy clothes and pretended to eat by hiding food in my napkin to be thrown away later. Even so, they still watched me like a hawk. Finally I moved out of my parents house when I was eighteen and was free to eat any way I wanted to. I could not stand* not *to be "in control" of my body, my food, or my life. I am now twenty-five years old and I've been in the*

hospital four times. The last time I almost died of a heart attack. I weighed seventy pounds.

—Emily

Girls and women start to starve themselves for many different reasons. Like Emily, some women feel unsafe at their natural weight and feel more secure about themselves the thinner they become. The anorexic gets panicky when she is not in control or not perfect, which manifests in her insistence on maintaining her weight below her natural weight. She experiences an unrelenting and intense fear of gaining weight. Often the anorexic looks into the mirror and instead of seeing an emaciated woman she sees someone who is fat. Her own self-perceptions are distorted and she often has feelings of self-hatred and disgust. When an anorexic first starts dieting, she often gets a lot of positive feedback, from friends, family, and the culture. Sometimes it is only after she has lost 10 to 20 percent of her natural body weight that anyone starts to get worried. This is too late—she is already hooked on the anorexic way of life: fasting, obsessive exercising, control. Her recovery depends on being willing to let go and trust her body and her feelings, love herself as she is, and tap into her own will to live. These are women whose obsessions are killing them.

I began dieting at thirteen and started throwing up at sixteen, after I saw another friend do it. At first it was just something I'd do now and then, after I'd eaten too much or when I felt too fat. But soon it seemed like I was eating too much too often and feeling fat all the time. In college I started running to try to keep my weight down, but I couldn't stop eating. The academic and social stress was just too much for me. I remember at night going from vending machine to vending machine, trying to fill this insatiable need to eat, and then feeling so disgusted afterward I would find the nearest bathroom and throw up. Only then would I feel calm enough to sit down and study. Soon it became a way of life for me, and I was throwing up three to four times a day. I lived with hatred and disgust with myself for this behavior, but there was nothing I could do to stop it. I would begin every day by telling myself that I was going on a diet and would stop eating and then wouldn't have to throw up. I would end every day by hating myself for all the food I ate, for all the times I threw up, and for how fat my body was. I was in the middle of a destructive, depressing cycle and couldn't see my way out.

—Laura

Like Laura, many bulimic women started purging after they had "failed" at dieting. They either felt they were eating too much, or their body was too fat, or both. Laura began purging by throwing up, and then began overexercising as a way to get rid of the food and weight. Other women use laxatives, diuretics, enemas, other medications, or fasting as a way to purge. Purging usually occurs after a binge in which a large amount of food is eaten. However purging can occur anytime and is frequently a response to overwhelming feelings. For the experienced bulimic, just the feeling of even small amounts of food in the stomach can trigger the need to purge. The binge/purge cycle itself can be self-perpetuating because the shame and anger from purging can create the need to soothe oneself with food, creating another binge that once again needs to be purged. Bulimic women, like their sister anorexics and compulsive eaters, usually spend a lot of time being concerned with their food and their weight. And like their sisters, bulimics also tend to have difficulty not only soothing themselves emotionally but containing and processing overwhelming feelings. In recovery, bulimics must learn to sit with the feelings, the fullness, and the weight without purging, and also learn to take care of themselves emotionally without using food.

LISA'S, EMILY'S, AND Laura's stories are not uncommon among women with eating disorders. Eating disorders are heartbreaking and fill people with despair. However there is a cure and it is powerful: to listen to what your eating problem is trying to tell you is the way through to the other side of your disorder. This process is what we call *going beyond hunger,* to achieve freedom from your overeating, the diet/binge cycle, and self-starvation.

We are writing this book to say *there is another way.* True recovery, going beyond hunger, is not a process of abstaining but of developing a self-assurance so that you choose what is best for your own unique body. It is a process of reaching deep into your own insatiable emotional and spiritual hunger, that which you have been trying to satisfy with food. It is looking at your eating disorder as a friend instead of an enemy, letting it teach you who you are and what you want from life. It is healing your relationship not only with food, but with yourself and your spirit. What we're proposing is not a quick fix. In some cases it can be a long and challenging path because of the depth of the transformation that is required. But one thing is certain, if you choose to undertake this path it will change your life forever.

Moving beyond hunger is a highly individualized process, one that is different for everyone. Our eating disorders are a reflection of our different histories, different ways we've been wounded by our culture or families, different experiences with controlling our weight and food, and different emotional and spiritual needs. For one person, it was the pain of always being overweight as a child and having her family and peers constantly teasing and judging her. For another it was the pain of always having to have a perfect body, but never being seen for who she really was. In both cases, the eating disorder was a reaction to the inner self being ignored, invalidated, and certainly not nurtured. Although the core issues may be the same, the process of recovery, like the process of wounding, is very different. You are the best judge of what you need for your healing. This book will help you learn how to heal.

As we know from our own experiences and that of the women we have worked with, struggles with food and weight can take us to the very core of our being. These struggles help us to find a peaceful relationship with food and our bodies. But they also show us how to reclaim our spiritual selves and our sacredness.

This book is about women who have lost their souls by becoming estranged from their passions, their truths, and their voices. It's about women who have strayed far from their paths and have gotten onto journeys that have no soul and no ending—a circular path that gets them nowhere. It keeps them locked in a destructive pattern and there is no way to reach any place of power or forward movement. This is a familiar place for women in our culture since women have been stuck there for many, many years. Women who are struggling with weight and food issues stand at the threshold of an emerging new vision of what it means to be a woman in the twenty-first century. And as long as the issue of weight is treated as purely a behavioral issue, isolated from the cultural and spiritual oppression of women, it will never be healed and our society will never evolve from this dysfunctional place.

This book is about being released from the struggle with food in whatever form that takes; either overeating, undereating, or obsessing. It is about discovering the emotional, physical, and spiritual issues that lie at the core of the eating disorder. It is about reclaiming our basic right to have desire and passion, to embody it and express it, and to manifest or create what we need. It's about having choice based on internal guidance—having the right to choose what we feel is right for ourselves and learning to hear the voice within that knows what we need. This book is about stepping out from under the oppression of body shame and body hatred, to reclaim once and for all our right to be a goddess.

Living a life beyond hunger means finding true recovery. Recovery means no more obsession about food and weight. Recovery means knowing who you are and what you want, and being able to communicate those desires. Recovery is knowing that you have a right to be here and take up as much space as you do. You no longer have to make your body get so small as to disappear or to get so big that you are sure to be seen. There *is* an alternative. You can start speaking with your voice instead of your body. Recovery is being proud of the size you are, the age you are, the color you are, the sex you are, and the person you are. Recovery is getting your life back, being your own true self, and living life to its fullest.

Chapter 2

LETTING GO OF JUDGMENT

Those who are without compassion cannot see what is seen with the eyes of compassion.

—Thich Nhat Hanh, *The Miracle of Mindfulness*

In order to recover from an eating disorder it is important to become conscious of what we are doing. Because this can be a difficult and painful process, it is imperative that we first learn to let go of the judgments we have against ourselves. When we begin to develop compassion for ourselves we also begin to understand that our eating disorders come from a deep, sacred place within us. Our eating disorders are the voices of our souls crying out to be heard. It is absolutely critical to understand: *You are not using food because you lack control, are undisciplined, or are flawed, but because it is the only way you can take care of yourself for now.* With time, you will be able to learn new ways to take care of yourself.

COMPASSION

From the time I was six to the time I was twelve I would steal candy from the kitchen and hide it in my room. There it would stay, safely hidden, until one of those awful days would hit—the day when my father would lose it and go into a rage, hitting everything and anyone in his way. It was on these days that my brother and I would retreat to my room, find my stash, and slowly, piece by piece, devour my candy. With each piece I would steadily become calmer and calmer, the terror and the pain slowly retreating. I don't know what I would have done without that candy—I think I would have died.

—Myra

In our groups and workshops we have heard story after story of women using food, and the obsession with food and weight, to cope with stressful situations as children, adolescents, or adults. The stories are different for everyone. For some it's because at an early age they were taught that how they looked was who they were, and they had to be thin to be okay. For some it might have been serious physical, emotional, or sexual abuse. For others it may have been growing up in a family or culture that didn't teach them how to cope with difficult feelings but taught them, for example, simply to "stuff" their hurt feelings or fears instead of expressing them in ways that could bring healing and comfort. What the exact story is doesn't matter. What matters is that we learn to listen to our own voices and hear our own stories.

I had been going to individual therapy for a while for anorexia. My therapist and I had been focusing on allowing me to eat more and to control my weight by swimming instead of not eating. Every week I would check in and report how much I ate and how much I swam. However hard I tried, I could not allow myself to eat more. I felt so much shame that I couldn't eat that I would come to therapy and lie about how much I ate.

—*Jill*

When Jill couldn't let herself eat, she began blaming herself, feeling even worse because she was too lazy and incompetent to follow the therapist's instructions. Many weeks later, after hearing the other group members share some of their feelings, we asked Jill what she thought her eating disorder was trying to say to her. She burst into tears and began talking about being depressed, lonely, and confused. She began to link these feelings to how she felt about her body and eating. Jill felt so much relief when she realized that there was an important reason why she was hating her body and not eating. Although she was just beginning the healing process, she was light-years ahead of where she had been because she finally heard the voice of her eating disorder that had been trying to tell her about her pain.

In order to heal you must be able to listen to your needs and passions. Your eating disorder originally comes from a profound place of strength, not weakness. It carries a very important message. Listen carefully to its voice. You may not know exactly what that message is right now—sometimes it takes a long time to hear it. But be patient with yourself. Trust and have faith that there is a good reason why you have issues around food. Honor and respect your eating disorder as a way you devised, early in life, for taking care of yourself. You didn't know any other way at the time. It was the only door you could find that wasn't closed to you. Admire the tenacity of your eating disorder—how it holds on and on and on until you have to listen. Trust that this will always lead you back to your own truth. It is truly a gift to be cherished. The foundation for recovery lies in creating compassion for your struggle and learning gratitude for how your eating helps you to survive. You can then start letting go of the binding shame, the self-judgment, and the self-hatred, that you have carried for years.

❂

THE FOLLOWING IS the first of many imagery exercises in this book. Imagery can be a powerful tool because it allows us to go inside ourselves and find our own unique truth. Like any skill, it can take time and practice to develop, so be patient. The first few times you do it you may not get any images. But keep at it and slowly they will become clearer. For some people imagery is not a useful tool, and if this is true for you, don't worry. Not every method works for everyone. We suggest that you read this exercise into a tape recorder so that you can lie down, close your eyes, and just listen without having to read the text. It may take some experimentation, and a few re-recordings to get the right pace for you.

Creating Compassion

Get into a comfortable position and, if you'd like, close your eyes. Bring your awareness to your breathing. Notice what it feels like to breathe in through your nose, down into your lungs and belly, and back out again. Pay attention to the sensations. Use your breath to bring your awareness into your body and away from your busy mind and all the stresses of the day. Just notice the natural rhythm of your breathing—don't try to change it. Notice the rising and falling of your belly and chest. Scanning from your head all the way down to your toes, notice if you are holding tension anywhere in your body. Maybe your shoulders are tense, or your belly, or your thighs. Breathe into the tension, imagining that you are sending relaxing oxygen to those areas. As you breathe out release any tension that you may be holding, allowing your whole body to relax. Let the couch, the floor, or the earth completely support you. There is nothing that you have to hold up. With each breath allow yourself to move deeper into your Self, deeper into that place within you where you hold your wisdom, deeper into your own truth.

From this place, remember a time when you first started over- or undereating. You may get a real memory, or an image that you've created. Just allow the picture to become clearer. Notice where you are. What are your surroundings like? What does it smell like? What kinds of noises are there? Can you see yourself? How old are you? What are you wearing? Watch the scene and notice your behavior. What are you doing with the food? Take as much time as you need to let the picture become clearer.

Now notice what you are feeling in the image. Are you angry, frightened, stressed, confused, excited? If this is hard for you to see clearly, ask the image to give you a further clue. Look closely. Or you might notice what you are feeling in your own body right now as this image comes up for you.

Now listen carefully, listen for the message of the eating disorder. What is your over- or undereating saying? Ask it directly if you'd like, asking the behavior in the image what is it doing and what does it want? Why is it here? Maybe it is trying to protect you from pain. Maybe it is trying to comfort you at a time when you are scared. Listen for the answer. You may see it, you may hear it, or you may feel it. Or you may get nothing. That is okay, too.

As you are looking at the image, try to feel compassion for yourself as you are behaving this way. Talk to yourself as kindly as you can, acknowledging the behavior and that it is there for a very important reason. You will eventually know the reason, whether or not you know it now.

When you feel complete, bring your awareness back to your breathing. Notice what you are feeling in your body. Breathe into the areas that feel tense and as you breathe out release the tension. With each breath, breathe in refreshing and awakening energy, and feel yourself slowly coming back to the room. When you're ready open your eyes.

UNDERSTANDING OUR INNER CRITICS

Shame kills faster than disease.

—BUCHI EMECHETA, *The Rape of Shari*

When I started listening to the things I would say to myself inside my head, I realized that one saying kept coming up over and over again: "You're too fat to play with us." When my therapist asked me where that saying came from, I realized that I was told that as a child by the other kids at school. It became the theme of my life. When every picture of a model in a magazine was thinner than I, I would say to myself, "See? You're too fat to be attractive." When I would go on an interview for work I would say to myself, "See? You're too fat to work for them." It became my whole identity—who I was in relationship to the world—too fat. I began to hate my fat, hate my body, and hate myself.

—Marie

Many women know the pain of self-hatred. It's a pain so deep and so insidious that it can be paralyzing even to begin to feel it. Where does the hatred come from? From the instant we are born, our perception of ourselves is influenced by the way our caregivers mirror back to us who we are. If a mother looks at her child with loving eyes and sees the beautiful being within the body, the child will experience the feeling of being loved and being seen. If a mother looks at her child with critical eyes and focuses only on the bodily imperfections, then the child learns to look at herself in the same manner. As children enter the school system, their peers have another profound impact on how they perceive themselves. Children who are teased because they are different (overweight, different ethnicity, disabled, etc.) incorporate these negative messages into their developing sense of self. As we become older and are exposed to the media, the messages that we receive from the culture also shapes the development of who we are and what we *should* be like. And of course for women, the most frequent and obvious messages we receive are critical of our bodies and completely neglect our spiritual selves. It's no surprise that the inner voice most women hear as strongest are the voices saying they are too fat, too tall, too flat, too big, too wrong. Our loving and spiritual voices become completely buried beneath the onslaught of these negative cultural messages.

These messages and the body hatred we have integrated into our own thoughts and feelings start to affect everything we do and everything we feel about ourselves. Our inner critical voice attacks not only our body but our mind and soul as well. Self-esteem, self-trust, and self-love erodes. The hatred we feel for our bodies soon permeates our whole being.

Your inner critic is a powerful force beneath your eating disorder that can be very old and very complex, incorporating all of the many messages you have received over time. In order to recover it's necessary to begin to listen to this voice and try to understand where you learned these negative messages and how you can begin to change them.

BECOMING A NONJUDGMENTAL OBSERVER

All day long, every day, I would mentally scream at myself for my weight and my eating. I never realized how cruel I was to myself. I wouldn't speak to anyone else that meanly. It was the way I heard my father speak to my mother all of my childhood. It was the way my mother spoke to herself when she looked in the mirror. I was sure it was the way others were silently speaking to me at all times.

— *Pam*

To let go of self-judgment, it is important to learn how to observe yourselves without the shaming voices that you have internalized.

As you begin to become aware of your habits, the first response is usually critical and negative. You developed this habit of critical self-talk through your life experience. You were not born with this habit. You learned it and can therefore unlearn it.

As Pam worked on her own critical self-talk she realized how many shaming words, sentences, and sayings were part of her everyday life. She started tuning in to this constant stream of negativity and little by little turned her attention to the challenge of changing the patterns of abuse she had internalized. When she found herself yelling at herself for overeating, she tried to get in between herself and the yelling long enough to really figure out why she was upset. When she started comparing herself to others—and nearly always coming up short—she tried to figure out other ways she was feeling "less than." When she found herself blaming all of her unhappiness on her body, she tried to go beyond the blame and discover the true source of her unhappiness, her childhood wounds.

Pam was taught to feel bad about herself and her body in her childhood. Because she was a "chubby child," she often heard that she had "such a pretty face" and if she would just lose a few pounds then her Mom would be happy, her Dad would be happy, and she would be happy. This taught her to blame her body for everything that went wrong in her life. Because she felt that every problem and every upset was due to her size, she never got to see what the normal challenges of growing up were all about. As she matured she continued to believe that if she would just lose some weight, then her life would run smoothly. It was only after she started to recover that she realized what a wonderful scapegoat her size had always been. She had to learn how to look beyond her issues with her body and work instead on the many issues hidden underneath.

RECOGNIZING THE DIFFERENCE BETWEEN JUDGING AND OBSERVING

In order to learn to observe my own behavior, so that I might someday be able to change it, I first had to develop a nonjudgmental observer within myself. In order to do that I had to become my own science experiment. This allowed me to step back and get a perspective on my eating disorder that I didn't have before. When I applied this to my food I was able to find out what foods I liked and didn't like. I found that sometimes I could eat ice cream and be fine and sometimes I would eat it and I would get a headache. I found out what the differences were for those times and what I could do about it. I found that I liked salads and "good foods" and I also liked french fries and "taboo" foods. By just observing and not judging, I learned to check with my body and not with society's rules about what I liked and did not like.

—*Jennie*

In order to recover you need to become your own science experiment and begin to notice when some things work better than others. It means knowing how to ask questions and being open to hearing the answers that come from deep within you. If you eat more than you are hungry for, observe how that feels *inside*. If you eat something that is too rich or does not agree with you, observe how that feels *inside* your body. No name calling, no shame, no punishment. You are learning, exploring, experimenting. When a scientist mixes together a formula A and B and gets a certain reaction, she doesn't criticize the formula for behaving this way. Instead, she says, "Isn't this interesting? What makes A and B react this way?" You need to develop a part of yourself that can observe and question your behaviors with this same sense of detachment and curiosity, without judging them—and only then can you really be safe enough to see the truth. No matter what you uncover, be it the way you look or the way you obsess about food, or anything else, repeat this simple phrase: *"Isn't that interesting?!"* This helps to take the charge out of what you've discovered and reminds you that you are trying to objectively observe yourselves.

> *When I was bingeing and dieting, I had no clue of what I really needed. I wasn't just a mouth, just a belly, just a bottomless hole to be filled. I had to see that I was so much more than my body, more than my eating disorder, more even than my feelings, thoughts, desires, and needs. Going beyond the hunger led into a small place that continued to lead into a much bigger place. The longing for that which I did not know, the heartbreak of always wanting something, was replaced with the deep understanding, love, and respect of what is.*
>
> —*Laurelee*

Meet each hunger with a sense of wonder and openness. It's a trick to learn how to do this, but it works! Imagine that you are your own best friend telling you something about yourself and telling you in the gentlest, most loving way possible. For instance, if you really wanted to know what a friend wanted for dinner, you would ask, then wait for the answer. You wouldn't demand that she eat what you tell her to eat and then call her a fat pig after all that food went to her hips. If you did, you would not have that friend for very long. But this is exactly what we do to ourselves several times a day, around each meal, for years and years. It takes time, trust, compassion, and a willingness first to ask, second to wait, and third to listen to the answer *without judgment* and without argument. We need to become our own best friends so that we can perform the holy and sacred act of breaking bread with ourselves.

Letting Go of Judgment

In this exercise we will work on letting go of judgment. Not an easy task! The important thing to remember is just to be aware. This is the time to become your own science project. We're asking you to go beyond the shame and self-hatred for your eating disorder and your body and become your own nonjudgmental observer. Only then can you find out where these judgments come from and only then will you be able to let those judgments go. It might help you to keep a journal about any questions that come up for you in this process. Then throughout the day write out any answers or insights that come up. Do not judge yourself for not doing this exercise perfectly; however you do it is the way you are supposed to do it. Keep reminding yourself to keep an open attitude of discovery. You are meeting the part of yourself that overeats, undereats, obsesses about her body constantly, controls her weight, or keeps weight on. You are on the path of learning who you are as a natural eater.

Note that this exercise is divided into three steps. You can take these steps at any speed you like. However, we recommend that you give yourself at least a couple of days on each step. Some women need more time, some less. However you do it is up to you—just trust your own pace.

Step One:

Be aware of your own judgments about your body. Where did you get these judgments? From your parents, the media, your peers? Where? In what ways is it in your own best interest to believe in the judgments you have of yourself?

What happens if you eat certain foods? Does your self-esteem go up? Or does your sense of self-worth plummet?

What happens to you if you feel thin? What happens to you if you feel fat? What if your pants are loose? What if your waistband is tight?

Start to notice the world in which you live. What kind of judgments do others have about your body, your eating, or their own bodies and eating?

Step Two:

How often today did you mentally scream at yourself, especially about how you ate or how you looked? Or what you did or did not do?

How often did you compare yourself to others and found yourself "not as thin, not as smart, not as beautiful, not as young, or not as good?"

Who in your life talks to you that way? Or talks to themselves that way? Who in your past talked to you that way? Or talked to themselves that way? Where did you learn it?

Step Three:

When you are aware that you are judging yourself, stop and try to create a newer, nonjudgmental voice. This is the voice that is your curious observer, the scientist. It just wonders with interest what you are doing. It may say "How does my body feel when I eat this food?" instead of "I'm bad for eating this food!" It may say "This is what my body looks like today," instead of "I'm so fat and disgusting!" It may say "Isn't it interesting that I'm eating when I'm not hungry?" instead of "I can't believe I'm such a pig!" With time your nonjudgmental voice will become stronger and easier to hear.

ACKNOWLEDGING THE PROGRESS IN TERMS OF HOLISTIC GROWTH

I had a very hard time grasping the concept that recovery meant so much more than weight loss. It took a long time for me to not want to measure my happiness and peace of mind by how much I weighed. It also was the first thing that people asked me about as I got better. Just because I wasn't crazed about my body, everyone assumed that I had lost weight, but the lightness that I was feeling would not show up on a scale. What people were noticing was that the heaviness of the obsession with food and the unrelenting desire to be thin was being lifted, not the pounds.

—Dana

This culture often measures the health of an individual by the way their bodies look. If they fit the mold of what society thinks is healthy and beautiful then these people are judged "good." If, however, they are fatter, thinner, shorter, taller, or are somehow different than the norm, then these people are judged "bad." We still unconsciously judge ourselves and others in this way, even though we may wish our society was more tolerant of peoples' differences. In recovery it's important to begin looking at ourselves in a holistic way, a way that includes our entire being, taking each part of ourselves into consideration.

I always judged my progress by weight loss. If I was losing weight I was successful, progressing, and on the right track. It didn't matter how crazy or unhappy I was. And if I was gaining weight at all, even a pound, I became a miserable failure. I could've been receiving the most prestigious honor for my work but it didn't matter—inside I was worthless.

—Sarah

As women we have been conditioned to judge our worth not only by our weight, but also by the progress of how much weight we've lost. How many of us can remember standing in the circle of women in a weight-loss program with everyone clapping because we had lost a pound that week! We could have been dying on the inside but it didn't matter—we had lost that pound and that was success. Judging ourselves in terms of weight loss only invalidates all the other extremely important emotional and spiritual foundation work that we could be doing.

We are taught in our culture to measure progress by the goals that we reach, not by the integrity and magic of the process itself. Yet it is here, in the process itself, the day-in, day-out reflections of who we are, that miracles happen. Focusing on our weight and the way we eat is only one small piece of the puzzle. Instead of abstaining from food, we heal our relationship with food and choose what is best for our own unique body. Instead of exercising to lose weight, we start to move our bodies because it feels good to move. We begin to reach deep inside ourselves and discover our real hunger, our emotional and spiritual hunger.

For each of us, that particular inner hunger is different. It may be a hunger to live our own lives, to express our own inner voice. It may be a hunger to love and be loved. It may be a hunger to claim our own power. This is profound and deep work and it is why we call it a holistic recovery. It works from the inside out. It works with our wholeness rather than with our fragments. We go within to our own truth, and there we find our true selves and our true voice. This is the healing we have been waiting for. And guess what? You had it within you all along.

People talk about their illness being lifted one day and I'm sure that is true for them. But for me it was a process of day-in and day-out work. One day I remember being able to say no to a friend. That was amazing for me. Another day, with my heart beating like a drum, I was able to ask my doctor not to weigh me. Months later I could touch my stomach with my hands and actually feel compassion for it. And eventually, years later, I could look in the mirror and respond to myself with love. One day I noticed that my body was changing—but it hardly seemed as important to me anymore. I had already transformed.

—Carol

We have witnessed women standing in front of a mirror and *for the first time in their lives* being able to feel and express love for themselves, and then the next week turn around and say, "I'm completely stuck. I'm not losing weight." We have seen women grow and change in beautiful and powerful ways but completely invalidate their growth because they haven't lost weight. Complete recovery from an eating disorder requires spiritual and emotional growth. Sometimes weight loss accompanies this growth, sometimes weight gain accompanies it, and sometimes no physical change accompanies it. The complete healing process is not linear. It can fluctuate and it is different for everyone. We will talk more about this later. But for now it's important just to understand that when we measure our progress only in weight loss or gain we set ourselves up for failure. There are three reasons for this: 1) We are not placing value on our spiritual and emotional recovery, which means we are not hearing the message of our eating disorder; 2) we have removed ourselves from being present with the internal process that is necessary for recovery; and 3) when we aren't gaining or losing weight at a regular rate, we think we've failed and we turn back to overeating or undereating.

I can't believe how many times I would jump on that scale, then jump right off and go directly for the food. I didn't stop to think what might be driving me to the food. If I had gained any weight at all it meant I wasn't doing it right—I was blowing it. I was "having a slip" or "falling off the wagon." I began to obsess about how fat I was getting, moving further away from what I needed at that time. How many times had I heard that all it takes is one slip and you are worse off than you were before? The pressure and the fear were unbearable. I can't believe how much relief I felt when I began to realize I didn't have to judge my healing by the scale.

—Trish

It is extremely important at this point to understand that we are not saying you have to be a weight that is not right for your body. We understand very well the implications and complications of being "overweight" or "underweight." But what we are saying most emphatically is that if you have an eating disorder and losing or gaining weight is your only measure of success, it will impair your ability to reach *true* recovery—and you will miss the many miracles along the way.

Acknowledging the Progress in Terms of Holistic Growth

Try to notice how often you measure your progress by your weight or looks. Ask yourself the following questions:

Do you feel the need to weigh yourself to find out how well you are doing? What happens if you've lost weight? What happens to your peace of mind if you haven't, or if you've gained a few pounds?

Where did you learn to measure yourself in pounds only? Is this the true measurement of your personality, your intellect, your body, and your soul? Can you come up with other ways to acknowledge your progress without focusing on your weight?

Begin to trust everything you do. Trust the way you eat and the way you think about food. Trust that your present weight is the perfect weight for where you are right now in your life. Trust that you have been trying to get your own attention for some time and now that you have it, promise yourself that you will continue to give it, unconditionally. Trust that you are doing the best you can.

BY FINDING COMPASSION for yourself and for your eating disorder you are laying a foundation of love and trust that will carry you throughout the rest of your recovery. By letting go of your shame and self-judgment you will be able to tolerate going beneath the symptoms of your eating disorder to listen to the needs of your body and soul. It's sort of like giving yourself the oxygen tank before you go deep-sea diving. Your compassion and nonjudgmental observer will help you feel safe enough to explore the depths of your soul.

Chapter 3

BECOMING CONSCIOUS

Oh, The glory of growth, silent, mighty, persistent, inevitable! To awaken, to open up like a flower to the light of a fuller consciousness!

—Emily Carr

I would wake up, as if from a dream, and find myself in the kitchen, with empty wrappers, cartons, and boxes of food all around me. "Oh, no, not again," I would groan. I felt that a monster had been let out, had been loose in my house, and had taken me prisoner. Immediately the shame, despair, and disgust would set in, as I once again came to realize that the monster was me. The only thing that would make me feel better was the sheer conviction that tomorrow I would put that monster on a very restrictive diet and by doing that this binge would be wiped out. Then many times I would have to eat throughout the rest of the day because I was scared of the deprivation I was going to be in. This happened to me again and again.

—Ilene

The experience of waking up after a binge and finding themselves in the midst of the evidence is a very common experience for women with eating disorders. This is what we call *going unconscious.* This means that at the exact moment we are eating, we are not aware of our actions, emotions, sensations, and thoughts. With eating disorders there are many ways of going unconscious, some more severe than others. Some women experience a "blackout," and literally can't remember what happened. Other women can remember what happened once they look back at their behavior, but they are not aware of it while it's happening.

Because the roots of eating disorders usually stem from patterns of behavior women have learned in the past, most of these actions, thoughts, and feelings related to eating disorders are unconscious. Women are often not aware of the physical cues of hunger or fullness. Women are often not aware of how frequently they think that they are "too fat." Many times they have no idea what they are feeling or that they even have such feelings at all. Actions, thoughts, feelings, and bodily sensations tell you what you need to do to heal yourself. So in order to recover completely you need to become aware of these signals.

Recovery is much more than stopping the obsession with food and weight. If it were only that, we certainly would not be writing this book. We struggled for years with this issue while gaining and losing the same pounds over and over. For us, learning to listen to ourselves and understand the roots of our own unique eating disorders was the only way out of this destructive cycle. When we awaken to ourselves exactly as we are in the present moment we can finally begin to listen to the voice of the eating disorder.

COMING OUT OF DENIAL

And the day came when the risk to remain tight in a bud was more painful than the risk it took to blossom.

—Anonymous

In the peak of my eating disorder I was eating vast amounts of food, throwing up six times a day, and totally obsessed with my weight. Yet if anyone had confronted me I would have denied it with passion—to them and even to myself. You see, for me to admit I had such a problem would've destroyed me because I had so much shame, self-hatred and disgust. The truth was just too frightening. Then one day someone very close to me that I loved and respected got into recovery and told me that they had a problem. A huge black cloud lifted that day. If someone I loved could have a problem then maybe it was okay if I had one. It gave me the strength to look at myself.

—Carol

Becoming conscious can be overwhelming, because there is so much shame attached to eating disorders, about the eating, starving, or purging, about your bodies, and about not being able to control yourself. Some of the shame comes from being told over and over again that all you need to do is just *eat the right food and exercise*—so you wonder, "What's wrong with me?" Some of the shame you experience comes from a culture that only values certain types of bodies. So if yours doesn't fit that mold you start feeling ashamed, rejected, or disapproving of yourself. One way or another you develop a perception that something is wrong with your body. Sometimes the shame you experience comes from events in your own childhood. But wherever it comes from it is always linked to the eating disorder. To acknowledge the depth of your eating disorder means you also have to feel the pain of shame, disappointment, disapproval—and this is hard to do. Sometimes it is so hard that to avoid these feelings you go into denial.

Denial can be a wonderful coping mechanism. It keeps us from seeing the truth when the truth is too devastating to face and protects us when we can't cope with all the uncomfortable feelings that often come with hard truth. Yet when we become conscious, we have to come out of denial, look straight into the heart of our eating disorder, and get to know it and ourselves on an intimate level.

In order to come out of denial it is important to keep practicing compassion and letting go of harsh self-judgments; if not, the rest of the process will be too painful.

BECOMING AWARE OF EATING PATTERNS

Becoming aware of your own eating patterns is simply a matter of observing what you are doing around food. It is important to only *observe* your behavior in these first few days. When you try to change your eating patterns at the same time that you are trying to learn about them, you slow down the awareness process. Your energy is used up for dieting instead of looking clearly at what's going on around you and within you where food is involved. There are good reasons for eating the way you do, and now is not the time to change anything; only by observing can you understand what is driving you.

Each of us has a certain pattern we follow in our lives. We get up at a certain time in the morning. We have breakfast. We go to work. We work. We eat lunch. We work some more. We leave our jobs, go home. We have dinner. Sometimes we go to a movie, a party, the gym. Most of us don't vary our patterns a lot, though certainly new challenges or opportunities arise that cause us to shift our attention to other matters temporarily. When it comes to our most basic patterns, particularly those that involve eating, they become so automatic and seemingly *natural* that they almost become invisible to us. It's perhaps a little like walking: once we learn the pattern, we do it without thinking.

The steps for becoming aware of our patterns of eating are relatively straightforward. Awareness starts with paying attention to these three key areas:

1. When you eat: After work? During work? Nights? Weekends?
2. How you eat: While doing something else? While reading? While watching TV? Are you eating fast or slowly?
3. Where you eat: In you car? Standing in front of the refrigerator?

When You Eat

Let's look at an example of the first eating pattern, *when you eat* and *when you don't eat.*

Jane reported the following: "I found that I generally gorged myself on weekends, though I practically starved myself during the week. I ate in front of the TV or while reading. I ate in front of the fridge. I ate in the living room. At night in my bed, I ate until I fell asleep. I sometimes even ate on my way to the bathroom. I would purposefully not make any plans with any of my friends, so that I could eat."

One of the first things Jane had to do was to notice this behavior of hers and *not do anything to change it.* Once she became a nonjudgmental observer of her own actions, she was able to clearly see *when* she was eating. Then and only then would she be able to identify what she wanted to change. But change itself came later. If she had tried to change immediately, she would have recreated her dieting pattern and would then have set up a smoke screen blinding herself to the underlying reasons for overeating. At the point that she started becoming aware of *when* she ate, she also started getting some insights about *why*. This, of course, gets into feelings, which we'll discuss in a moment. For now, however, Jane's assignment was just to take note of *when* she was eating, the time of day she was eating and what type of trigger may have caused it, without trying to change that pattern or even probe the reasons why. Awareness, not change, was her goal.

We ask you to notice the *when* of your eating and often you will notice a trigger that goes with it. But instead of going numb or beating yourself up for your overeating, say to yourself, "Isn't that interesting! I'm eating all weekend long. I'm refusing to eat when I'm hungry. I'm eating after I get off the phone with my mother. I stop eating whenever I have a fight with my boyfriend. I'm eating when I'm upset that I'm eating. I'm eating at every coffee break. I'm eating every time I go to the movies." Again, we ask you not to change anything. We just want you to notice the times and the triggers of your eating.

How You Eat

The second eating pattern to notice is *how* you eat. Are you scarfing food down as fast as you can or are you meticulously picking at your food without really eating anything? Are you reading? Watching TV? Are you eating in front of others? Or do you never eat when someone else is around? Do you plan your evenings and weekends around your binges? Do you cook for everyone else but yourself? For example:

Marianne would only eat when doing something else, such as watching TV or reading. She never had a sit-down meal unless friends invited her out. Then she would only pick at her food, eating like a bird. When she got home she would head straight for the fridge and eat everything she could get her hands on, as fast as she could.

She knew that she was trying to distract herself by reading or watching TV. And she knew that she didn't want her friends to see how she ate. When she took a good look at her behaviors, she could then see *why* she did what she did. However her first step was to notice the *how* of her eating and then take it from there, later.

Again, the point is *not to change anything*, just to notice the patterns of what you do. Everyone has her own way of doing things. What is important is to recognize what your way is, nothing more. We will get into how to change those patterns later.

Where You Eat

The third eating pattern to notice is *where* you eat. Do you eat in the car, in the movies, at home, alone? Or do you eat in the mornings, at four o'clock at work, or as soon as you get home? Maybe you only eat late at night, in bed.

Susan is a good example. She would force herself to eat small amounts when she was around friends and family, but when she got home she wouldn't allow herself to eat anything, even if she was hungry.

Beth is another example. Her eating was tied to a specific place where she would overeat. She would eat no breakfast. Then she ate a very small diet lunch and dinner. After dinner, as the night wore on, she would get hungrier and hungrier and by midnight she would "wake up" in front of the fridge or over the sink. Many times she had no idea how much she ate, except by looking at the empty bowls, wrappers, or plates around her. She would also "space out" while driving from convenience store to convenience store, eating as much junk food as she could. Many times she went to the movies, just to be able to sit in the dark and binge on the popcorn and candy. She noticed that she always overate when she visited her parents, who still lived in her childhood home.

No matter how many times she swore she would not overeat in any of these places again, invariably she would once again find herself in front of the fridge or the sink, in her car, at the movies or at her parents' home, eating, eating, eating.

The first step in her recovery was to notice *where* she ate, and in so doing she was later on able to figure out *why*.

As they start on this program people think they are eating more than ever before. We hear over and over, "I'm getting worse, I can't believe how often I'm eating; how much I'm eating; or all the places where I'm eating!" But most of the time that's not true. What is true is that their awareness has increased, so it only seems as if they're eating more. This is common and to be expected if you are to become conscious of what you have been doing all along.

Feel free to do the exercises in this book at your own pace. It doesn't matter how slowly or quickly you get through them, how many of them you do, or how thoroughly you do them. Just notice your experience of them. The suggestions you find in the following exercises might trigger new realizations about your own truths, your own needs, and your own hungers. It is these truths, needs, and hungers that will take you to your own answers. It is often helpful to use a notebook or journal. Writing down what you are noticing might reinforce your observations.

Becoming Conscious of When, How, and Where You Eat

When you first get up in the morning, simply notice what you go for. Is it a cup of coffee? A sweet roll? Do you find yourself looking forward to cooking yourself a big breakfast? Do you eat on the run? Do you skip breakfast altogether, whether you are hungry or not?

What do you do once you've started your day? Do you have food nearby? In your car? In a drawer at work? Do you run down to the coffee shop or hit up the vending machines? Do you attend to your hunger or ignore it completely?

When do you eat lunch? What do you eat for lunch? Do you bring your own food or do you go out? With others or by yourself? Do you skip lunch, even if you are hungry?

What happens at four o'clock? Do you eat because it's coffee break time again and you don't know what else to do? Do you eat food you have stashed in your desk? Do you eat a snack when you bring the kids home from school?

Do you stop on the way home to buy groceries? Do you eat while you are shopping?

What happens to you once you come home? Do you head immediately to the kitchen for food or do you wait for dinner? When do you eat dinner and what do you eat? Do you eat fast to get it out of the way? Do you eat the same thing every night or do you like to make interesting and exotic meals? Do you take the time to eat slowly, to enjoy your meal? Do you eat alone or with others? Do you skip dinner?

Do you eat after dinner or get up late at night to eat? What kind of foods are you drawn to? Comfort foods? Sweets? Are you standing up or sitting down to eat? Do you go to bed hungry?

The most important thing is to observe and to notice, without judgment or blame. Don't get caught up in plans to change what you're discovering. For now, let it be as it is.

EMOTIONS

Next you try to become aware of your emotions associated with eating. If there's a single important principle to keep in mind here, it is this: The issue of food and weight is serving an important function in your life and you have no chance of letting it go until you understand what that function is. This does not mean that you have to understand every emotional reason why you are over- or undereating. But it does mean that you need to realize you've been trying to help yourself the only way you know how.

For example, Caryn discovered that if something was bothering her, many times she would turn to food. Food was always immediate, easy, dependable, and safe. She started to notice that she could count on food. She observed that food would numb her when she needed a break; it would help speed her up when she was tired; it would fill up a hole when she was feeling alone; and it would separate her from other people when she felt she needed protection.

She started to notice that even the binge cycle was aimed at taking care of her emotions. She became aware that many times as she swallowed her last bite of food, her utter self-hatred would set in. She could depend on that. As soon as these feelings of disgust set in, other feelings she wanted to escape from would disappear and she would know that the end of this binge was near. This was, in a strange way, the light at the end of the tunnel. It was a necessary part of the whole episode of overeating. It is important to understand this; *the pain of hating herself and beating herself up was easier to withstand than the emotional pain that she was trying to get away from in the first place.* Her self-hatred was familiar. She knew how to deal with it. This part of the dynamic of her eating disorder was very tenacious. It had been there a long time and had kept her safe from her feelings. It was not only the hardest to understand, but also the hardest to let go of.

In her recovery, Caryn started to see that each and every part of the eating disorder was her way of taking care of herself—the only way she knew at that moment. She feared that if she gave up her eating problem, her feelings would overwhelm her. If food was what worked, even only sometimes, what would she do without it? She had to find out that she could and would live through her own feelings.

She started to notice that when she took care of herself in ways other than with food she was answering her own call for help. Soon she was building self-trust. She started to trust that she would give herself what she needed most in the moment, such as support, love, and compassion. Once she knew that she could depend on herself to take care of herself, she no longer needed such drastic measures to get her own attention. She would acknowledge her feelings long before she was facedown in the pudding bowl.

Over time as she cultivated a strong observer self she gently and naturally started to change. This came later as her recovery unfolded. Until then she only made the agreement that she would notice when she was upset and then, as much as possible, feel her feelings. She didn't have to change anything; for now it was enough just to notice.

Becoming Aware of Emotions

Look at what happens the first thing in the morning. When you reach for the first food you will ingest, ask yourself "What am I feeling? How am I doing? Am I hungry?"

As you go through your day, keep asking yourself these questions. What is it about coffee breaks that makes you want to eat? Are you bored? Do you reward yourself with food?

Are you purposely withholding food from yourself? Does the thought of eating make you feel anxious? When you don't allow yourself to eat, how do you feel?

What about lunchtime? Do you look forward to eating, just getting through the morning until you are able to get food? Do you get anxious about eating in front of people? Do you hide in your office or kitchen?

Do you get overwhelmed, or filled with despair at the grocery store? Do you buy only what is "good" for you or do you rebel and buy only junk food?

What happens to your emotions when you get home? Do you find yourself eating as soon as you cross the threshold? Do you numb the stresses of your day with dinner? After dinner? Do you feel you need to eat everything to stop the feelings from coming up?

None of these uses of food is wrong or crazy. There is a very good reason for every bite you take. For the individual with an eating disorder, every unacknowledged feeling and problem has a way of turning itself into eating or controlling food. There was little else you could have done when you first learned these patterns. The way to recover is to notice, and in the noticing you ultimately discover a lasting solution.

BODY SENSATIONS

I had spent most of my life trying not to feel my body, because to feel my body was to feel the pain of my childhood. Starting when I was a child it was much safer to remain numb from the neck down. It was painful for me to zero in on my stomach, my chest, my heart. So when I started to try to become aware of my bodily sensations, at first it hurt and felt very strange. I quickly discovered that I kept most of my feelings in my stomach and chest. It took a long time to feel the difference between physical hunger and emotional hunger. I had restricted my food intake for so long, by dieting, that I had not a clue what my natural appetite was. I knew very well what I was supposed to eat to be healthy, when I was supposed to eat, and when I was supposed to stop. I knew this because I had been told over and over by diet experts, friends, family members, diet books, and articles in women's magazines. But I had no idea what I wanted to eat, when I wanted to eat, and when I wanted to stop. The truth was I knew all the answers, but didn't know the questions.

—Janet

Becoming aware of bodily sensations associated with eating is a special challenge for people with eating disorders. Many women have lost contact with the normal sensations and indicators of hunger, fullness, or feelings. Often they are not eating to satisfy hunger in the first place, and are dissociated from their bodies. They need to rediscover what hunger—*physical hunger*—is.

Like Janet, you have to let yourself feel your bodily sensations. You need to focus your attention on your body and notice when you feel something in your throat, your chest, your belly. When you feel these sensations ask yourself, "Am I hungry? What am I feeling? Am I upset? Am I tired?"

Of course, in the beginning you might not know the answers to these questions but with time the answers will come.

Becoming Aware of Body Sensations

Let yourself feel your own body. Where does your hunger lie? What is happening inside you as you reach for food? Does your stomach growl? Does it hurt? Some people feel a pressure in their throat or stomach. Some people feel an almost panicky sensation as they think about eating or not eating. Any and all body sensations are okay. The goal here is just to notice them.

THE DIET MENTALITY

Most people with eating disorders have deeply ingrained thought patterns about dieting and their bodies. For example, every time they put food in their mouths they are evaluating the amount of calories or fat grams they're taking in. They are fantasizing about how many pounds they will gain or lose. Every morning when they wake up and get on the scale, their attitude for that whole day might depend upon whether they've gained or lost a pound. They are constantly running their lives by dieting myths such as, "If I eat before I go to bed I will gain more weight." And most women are completely aware at every social event where the food is and how much of it they can or cannot eat. We call these thought patterns the "diet mentality" and we believe that almost every woman who has grown up in this culture has automatically learned to think this way. In fact, this thinking can become so obsessive and habitual that women with eating disorders spend huge amounts of time and energy living in the diet mentality without even knowing it. They get to the point that they consider it normal and natural. This diet mentality can literally consume whole lives.

For example, when Tina started becoming aware of her thinking about food, she could not believe how much time in her day it consumed. The first thing she thought of when she woke up was how much weight she either lost from dieting the day before, or gained from bingeing before she went to bed. She would make a promise about what she would or wouldn't eat that day. She'd calculate exactly how many fat grams she could have. Before each meal she would make sure she drank liquid (a dieting rule) and all day at work she would refill her water bottle to make sure she was drinking enough (another dieting rule). At the birthday luncheon for her co-worker, all she could think about was how she was not going to let herself eat a piece of cake because of the number of fat grams it contained. She realized she spent the whole luncheon obsessing about the food, and wasn't present. Often when she came home at night she would restrict her eating based on what she ate that day, and if she binged she would spend the whole evening planning her diet for the next day to make up for the binge. She made sure she didn't eat later than 7:00 P.M. (another dieting rule). By the time she climbed into her bed at night, she realized that most of her day was spent thinking about food.

In addition to becoming aware of thought patterns around diet, it's also helpful to become aware of thought patterns about your body. Women in our culture have learned to be extremely critical of their bodies and to have unrealistic standards of how their bodies should look. Many women constantly look in the mirror and judge themselves, many times even hating what they see. Part of becoming conscious is becoming aware of the level of self-hatred that you carry toward your body and how many times a day you say mean and critical things to your body.

When Gloria started listening to what she was thinking when she stood in front of the mirror, she was astonished by how much she hated herself. She found herself thinking things like, "You look disgusting this morning. Look at that fat stomach and those chunky cheeks. You are a gross, fat pig!" When she would catch a glimpse of herself in a store window she found herself saying, "Oh, my God! You are so flabby. Who would ever want to go out with you?" And whenever she saw a thin woman she would compare herself to her and wonder why she couldn't have her stomach, her thighs, or her breasts. She began to feel like a failure and a bad person whenever she ate. Gloria found that within moments of seeing her reflection she had spiraled into a deep sense of shame and depression. She was amazed to realize that this process happened about ten times a day.

When you start to become conscious of how much time and energy you are putting into thinking about food and your body, and how many uncomfortable feelings are connected with these thoughts, you may become overwhelmed. It is difficult to become aware, to realize how deeply entrenched you are in this battle with food. Sometimes it seems so much safer to stay in denial, to stay unconscious or to stay in a destructive pattern, but that's only because it's familiar. Only by becoming conscious, by watching and working with yourself in the moment, can you truly understand what you need to change.

Becoming Aware of Your Diet Mentality

Try to become aware of how many thoughts you have during the day that are related to dieting. Explore the following questions:

What is the first thought about food or weight that you have? Do you wake up wondering about how much you gained or lost? How often during the day do you think about how many calories or fat grams are in the food you're eating? How often do you feel guilty for eating something? How often do you feel in control, or proud of yourself for eating something or not eating something?

How often do you weigh yourself? How does weighing yourself affect your mood for the day? Do you plan to lose a certain number of pounds by a certain date or occasion?

What type of dieting myths do you live by? Do you find yourself doing certain rituals, such as always leaving one or two bites of food on your plate, or not eating after 9:00 P.M., because you think it will help you stay thin? How much time do you spend thinking about ways you can keep yourself from overeating?

How much time do you spend planning what you should eat? How much time do you spend thinking about what you already ate? How concerned are you about what other people think about what you are eating?

TRY TO BECOME aware of how many thoughts you have during the day related to your body and your looks. Notice how these thoughts make you feel. Explore the following questions:

What are you saying to yourself when you look in the mirror? Does it change at different times of the day? What about when you catch a glimpse of yourself in a window? How do you respond when you see yourself in a picture or video? How often do you compare yourself to other bodies? How often do you wish you had a different body part? How critical are you of other people's bodies when you are out in public? How much importance do you put on other people's looks? What is the first thing you notice about a person?

Do you have any positive thoughts or feelings about your body? How many times a day are you affected by negative thinking or feelings about your body?

As you continue to become conscious, increasing your self-awareness throughout each day, you will also become aware of the powerful and unrelenting impulse to judge yourself. Indeed there is a constant tug within us to put ourselves down every time our awareness awakens to some other way we're not *perfect*. This is quite natural and is part of the process. Be gentle with yourself. We are asking you to look directly into the face of your eating disorder with love, understanding, and compassion. This is not as easy to do as you might think, but it is possible one step at a time.

Chapter 4

HONORING THE PHYSICAL BODY

Bodies never lie.

—Agnes DeMille

The body has been made so problematic for women that it has often seemed easier to shrug it off and travel as a disembodied spirit.

—Adrienne Rich, *Of Woman Born*

Honoring the physical body means developing respect for our body's innate wisdom. Although it is absolutely necessary to work on the underlying emotional and spiritual roots of an eating disorder in order to recover, we believe it's important to start with the physical body itself. Many women who come to our groups are so disconnected from their bodies that they need to learn to be in their bodies before they can do the emotional and spiritual work. In addition, many women are in physical crisis. Their food and bodies feel either out of control or in danger and they are frightened. They need concrete tools to help them work with their over- or undereating and their bodies before they can concentrate on anything else.

By learning these tools it becomes easier to explore the emotional and spiritual issues because you are able to differentiate between what is physical hunger and what is emotional and/or spiritual hunger. Also, as you begin to use these tools, the underlying issues will begin to bubble up to the surface because now there is room for them. This process is by no means linear. We start with the physical but it will still need to be worked on as you move through the emotional and spiritual work. Exploring the emotional reasons why you eat will be more effective when you can tie it to the physical body. The process of recovery really involves working on all three issues simultaneously, because they are so intricately interconnected.

LISTENING TO THE BODY'S WISDOM

Many people can listen to their cat more intelligently than they can listen to their own despised body. Because they attend to their pet in a cherishing way, it returns their love. Their body, however, may have to let out an earth-shattering scream in order to be heard at all.

—Marion Woodman, *The Pregnant Virgin*

Automobiles need fuel to operate. Bodies need food to operate. But, unlike cars and gasoline, humans use food for more than just keeping the machine running. Women with eating disorders have relied on over- or undereating to solve many different problems in their lives. Over- or undereating for reasons other than hunger or fullness is not bad or wrong, it's just not always the best way to take care of ourselves. Initially eating or controlling food may dull the pain we're feeling and the weight gain or loss may insulate us from a threat. But over time the choice to use food in these ways becomes a source of pain in itself. It can block us from being able to recognize fully our real needs or how to satisfy them. When we can identify our physical, emotional, and spiritual needs and develop ways to satisfy them, then we can let our bodies return to their natural state of being. There is a beautiful Zen saying, "Eat when you're hungry, sleep when you're tired, and cry when you're sad." When we give ourselves permission to eat, to sleep, and to cry, we show incredible compassion and love for the one who needs it the most, ourselves.

> *My sister raised us two younger kids. My mom took a night job when I was a baby. The family needed more income and she went to work. She worked from 11:00 P.M. to 7:00 A.M. My father slept like a log. So who was feeding me? Babies eat five to seven times a night. I think it goes back that far for me. I think I went hungry a lot during that time.*
>
> —*Patricia*

When we came into this world, we came with a body that held all of the wisdom needed for development. A baby knows exactly when she's hungry, exactly when she's full and exactly what she likes and dislikes. When we are born, unless something is horribly wrong, we are born with automatic bodily functions: our hearts beat and our lungs breathe without being told to. Our body temperatures are self-adjusting. We sleep and we wake up. We know when we are hungry and we know when we are full. We know what nourishment we need and we demand it by crying. If our cries for food are fulfilled, we are satisfied. If not, we are unhappy and hungry and frightened. Regardless of whether or not we get fed, our baby bodies know what they need. Our appetites are inherent. Most babies do not need to be on a special diet; they do not need to weigh and measure their food, and they do not have to worry about tubby thighs.

With cultural and family pressures, we become less in touch with our innate wisdom, and more in touch with what we are told we *should* do: "Eat all the food on your plate," "You can't leave the table until you've eaten all your peas," "Don't spoil your appetite," "Eat three weighed and measured meals a day."

The way out of eating disorders is to believe our bodies when they tell us we are hungry, trust our bodies when they tell us what they want, have faith that our bodies know when they are full, listen to the inherent voice of our body's wisdom, and go as far back as we need to go to feed ourselves as if we were little babies. We have to give to ourselves now the amount of love and caretaking that we would give to our own children.

The first step in doing this is to give up dieting. Many, many books have been written about how diets don't work. Then they proceed to give you a "diet plan," a "lifestyle change of eating," or a "healthy choice." This is not giving up dieting! What we mean when we say give up dieting is actually to give up all the ways you are trying to exert control over what you eat. Let your body start dictating what it wants, when it wants it, and when it's had enough. This is called a natural way of eating.

Animals in the wild eat in a natural way. They know when they are hungry. They know which foods would be best for their bodies. They naturally know when they are full and they naturally know when to stop. They do not worry about counting calories or fat grams, or following the four-basic-food-group chart. They follow a natural appetite that keeps them at the right weight and size for their genetic heritage. Children who have not had their food and weight controlled by adults are also natural-born eaters. Children who are still in touch with their bodies' internal controls eat when they are hungry, and if they can get it they eat only what their bodies tell them to. They will also stop the moment they are full. Even at a party where cake and ice cream are served, they will only eat as much as they want. They don't care that they may never be at this party again, that they may never see this cake or this ice cream again. They trust that there will always be another party, a cake and ice cream. They do not have to eat it all now.

The distrust of your own body and your own appetite happens later. The attitude that you have to eat it all right now or that you can't eat any of it now comes only after years and years of deprivation, willful control, dieting, or not being able to eat what comes naturally for you. It comes after the silencing of the natural voice telling you that you are hungry and what you are hungry for.

When we return to this natural way of eating and listen to what we want and how much we want and when we want it, our freedom is at hand. We hear all the time the fear and disbelief that eating naturally is actually the way to recovery for eating disorders. But, remember, an eating disorder is *never about the food*, and you already know how to eat what you need. You were born with this knowledge. Now you need to give your body the trust and permission to reclaim your body's inherent wisdom. And then you need to follow *your* own instructions.

> *When I was born, the popular way to feed babies was by "timed feedings." This is when measured amounts of formula, at specific timed intervals, were fed to infants,* even if they cried for more*! I can remember being hungry all the time. As I grew up, I promised myself that I would never go hungry again. I was a "skinny" baby, but then I became a "chubby" child, a "large" teenager, and finally a "fat" adult. The next time my food was regulated was when I was put on a diet at the age of nine. Whenever I lost weight on a diet, (something I desperately wanted) I would immediately put it back on. It wasn't until I was starting to recover that I put my early starvation together with my needing to eat vast amounts of food.*
>
> *—Kay*

We know that giving up dieting and trusting yourself can be terrifying, that it goes against all that you have been conditioned to believe. But letting yourself eat as you want is a basic right that has been taken away from you. When you reclaim your right from the dieting experts, from your family and friends, but most of all from your *internalized diet adviser*, you will have found true freedom. When your food choices come from within, from your own body, your body will reach and remain at whatever is its correct weight. Trying to force your body to conform to an unnatural weight or size is possible only for a while and has negative consequences. Not only are you feeding the obsession to have the "perfect" body, you are setting the stage for the rebel within you to gain or lose weight in a way that might be unhealthy for your particular body.

Eating this way is a simple solution to a complex problem. But understanding the many different reasons we are doing the things we do around food and eating helps us to let go of the behavior that no longer serves us. Compulsive overeating comes from being afraid that there will never be enough. If we show ourselves, over and over, that not only is there enough, but that there is even more than enough, we've taken away at least one of the reasons to overeat. For the anorexic, giving up dieting can feel as if you will be out of control. But actually, as you learn to follow your bodily cues of hunger and fullness, you will be more in control of yourself, your body, and your soul. You will be in abundance rather than in deprivation.

> *When I first found out about eating when I was hungry, eating what my body wanted, and stopping when I was full, I was elated and hopeful. In all of my years of dieting I never listened to what I wanted. For the first six months, I followed these simple instructions and my body started to shift and change. As I went along, I started to lose a little weight, and then all of a sudden I wanted to lose more. I started to put pressure on myself to wait a while before eating. I started to try to only want "good foods" and I started to stop eating before I was truly satisfied. I had put myself on "the eat when you are hungry, eat what you want and stop when you're full" diet!! This, of course, did not work and within a very short period of time I was back in the obsession. I then had to stop trying to control my appetite, listen within, and eat as my body dictated.*
>
> *—Lisa*

It is common to want to return to dieting mentality. Most people do exactly that when they start working with these concepts. It is part of the process. The way to move beyond this diet mentality is to notice it and begin avidly seeking the wisdom of the body.

There are a few good books that explore in depth how to stop dieting and start eating from bodily hunger. If you find that, after you've read about eating when you're hungry, eating what you want, and stopping when you're full, you would still like more information to help you do this, we recommend Hirschmann and Munter's *Overcoming Overeating* and Geneen Roth's *Breaking Free from Compulsive Eating.*

How do you even begin to seek the wisdom of the body? You do it one step at a time—eating experience by eating experience. Every mealtime is another chance to feed yourself in a natural way, to take care of yourself as you have never done before, to love and trust yourself to nourish and answer your own call. This way of self-care moves out into all other areas of your life, but it starts with the precious act of feeding yourself meal by meal, day by day.

WHEN YOU ARE HUNGRY

At first I did not feel hunger. Only an underlying panic that I would never eat again. Or that I wouldn't do this "right." Or that once I started eating I would never stop. I was terrified of my "hunger." But as I just kept checking in and asking softly and politely, "Are you hungry, yet?" eventually I learned the signal of my own hunger.

—Amy

We hear over and over again, "But I'm always hungry!" or "I'm never hungry!" What is often the truth is that most women with eating disorders don't have a clue what their natural hunger is or how their natural hunger feels. This is the first step to eating when you are hungry. Let yourself get hungry. Wait to feed yourself until you get a clear physical message. For some women, this physical sensation is in their throat, for some it's in their chests, for some it's in their bellies. Some women get light-headed and spacey. Some women get tired and cranky. There are many, many ways the body tries to tell you it needs nourishment. The important thing to do is to listen and to start to learn your own signal. This might take a while and be very scary. You might feel out of control waiting for your body to tell you what to do. Your body doesn't run on clocks. It doesn't know that breakfast is at eight, lunch is at twelve, and dinner at seven. Chances are that your natural hungers won't be at any one of the culturally approved times. Be patient, you are meeting and getting to know who you are as a natural eater, someone that you may have forgotten. Rest assured that your body remembers, and if given the chance, it will lead you to food when it's ready to eat.

Eating When You're Hungry

1. Today, let yourself feel hunger. You may want to start this exercise when you don't have to go to work or at a time when you don't have any stresses on you. Try not to eat until you feel your own hunger. For now, forget about the "proper" times to eat and "approved" foods.
2. When you start to feel your hunger, notice everything about it. Where is your hunger? In your belly? In your chest? In your mouth? In your head? Try to stay with this hunger for as long as possible, until you get a really good idea of how it feels.
3. When you have felt your true hunger allow yourself to eat. Be aware of what it feels like to eat when you are hungry.

EATING WHAT YOUR BODY WANTS

I didn't know what I wanted. Once all food was "legal," I wanted everything and then I wanted nothing. When the "charge" of forbidden foods was gone, so was the obsession to eat them. When I wasn't on a "diet" anymore, "diet-type" foods became something I would eat if I wanted to and not eat if I didn't. It took some time before I was able to figure out what I wanted and then it took even more time to be willing to eat according to what my body told me to eat.

—Belinda

In this culture we are taught that there are bad foods and good foods. Then to make matters worse, of course, we perceive ourselves as bad or good if we eat these foods. This sets up numerous rules and regulations concerning what we should and should not eat. To try to weed out what society tells us about food and what our bodies tell us about food requires the radical approach of "legalizing" all foods. No food is bad, and no food is good. Candy, avocados, pasta, and celery are all equal. The only difference is how your own body feels after eating a particular food. This is the only diet rule we offer: What your body wants and how it feels afterward are the only measure you need.

In the past few years, we have seen major changes in the American diet. For some people these changes may be right, but for others they may be the worst thing possible for their unique body. People all over the world eat all kinds of foods, according to their own food supply, traditions, and genetic makeup. It is as ludicrous to expect these people to eat according to the "right way" (our way) as it is to expect all Americans to eat the "right way" (the same way). We are also all kinds of people with all kinds of different bodies and we ourselves are the only ones who can decide what is best for us.

The truth is that the "right" way changes all the time. Fifteen or twenty years ago, carbohydrates, like bread, potatoes, and corn were "wrong." Meat, cheese, eggs, and milk were what would "make your body strong." Then a few years later, meat and dairy were bad while pasta, vegetables, and beans were good. Right now, fat is bad, sugar is not exactly okay, but it's better than fat. From year to year research fluctuates and so do the opinions of the experts. This leaves the consumer confused about which foods they should or shouldn't eat. This is why we feel that our own bodies are the best at telling us what we should and should not eat, not the culture, not the "diet experts," not the television commercials and the magazine ads, and not our own minds that have been brainwashed on what is "good." We are not saying that nutritional and medical advice isn't important—it is extremely important—but it needs to be tailored to the individual's unique bodily response. Our bodies always give us the true and correct answer to the questions "What do I want to eat?" and "How does it feel in my body?" All we need to do is ask the questions and then listen for the answers.

Eating what you want is probably the most confusing part of listening to your body's wisdom. It's tricky because it takes time to learn the difference between what your body *wants* to eat, and what your mind thinks you *should* eat, or what your emotions are *driving* you to eat. When you keep paying attention to the subtle cues of your body, you can tell the difference. If you are experiencing undesirable symptoms from a certain food, such as headaches, stomachaches, rashes, fatigue, nervousness, foggy thinking, irritability, etc., these experiences are telling you something—trust it. If you think you might have an allergy, you may need the help of a professional to help sort this out. However, if you seek the advice of a nutritionist, allergist, physician, or some other specialist, we recommend that you find one that supports the nondiet approach, listens to your own unique body, and understands the complex issues surrounding eating disorders.

Legalizing food doesn't mean you have to eat everything. It just means that what you eat is *your* choice. When you stop defining a food as "bad" or "wrong" or "unattainable" or "fattening," you can start seeing it objectively as just another food with a certain shape, taste, and physical effect on your body. There is no emotional "charge" around foods anymore: nothing to rebel against, nothing to feel guilty about, nothing to get angry at. You are left with a more objective physical reality about how your body responds to certain foods. You can *choose not* to eat a certain food because it doesn't nurture you—not because you are bad or wrong or weak if you do eat it. And if you *do choose* to eat a certain food that doesn't agree with you, don't beat yourself up, but say to yourself, "Isn't this interesting? Why am I eating this when I know it will hurt me?" Ask yourself why you might want to feel the way that this food makes you feel. Why do you want to feel bad? Is it easier to feel the pain physically than to feel it emotionally? There may be some work here for you to learn how to stop hurting yourself and start nurturing yourself.

Some women in our groups legalize food by going to the store and filling their cupboards with everything they have previously defined as forbidden. By having an abundance of foods in their cupboards, they can allow themselves to eat these foods and figure out for themselves which foods they want, how much, and when. Some women feel too overwhelmed by this and need to legalize one food at a time. For those who have specific dietary restrictions based on medical necessity, it is important to find foods that you can eat and are satisfying to you so that you don't feel deprived. Deprivation is a common trigger for bingeing.

In recovery, the emotional and physical issues are so interconnected that it's very important to stay aware of your bodily feedback. Some women find that it's difficult to stop eating a certain food if they are emotionally distraught, and they need to work on the emotional issue first. Other women may find it helpful to first *choose not* to eat a certain food because their allergic reactions (i.e., rashes, congestion, fatigue, foggy thinking, headaches, etc.) prevent them from being able to focus on emotional issues. It is not a linear process, and you will find that you are working on both levels at once.

Once again, it takes practice, perseverance, and patience. But if you keep listening, you will find your own wisdom.

Eating Exactly What Your Body Wants

When you are in touch with your hunger, it is easier to know exactly what you want. Listen to the hunger closely and ask yourself these questions pertaining to food.

1. "What kind of food would most satisfy me at this moment?" Do not be concerned if at first you only want "forbidden" foods. If you have been in deprivation for a long time, the foods you have been depriving yourself of all these years may be the only foods it seems you want. Geneen Roth, in her book *Breaking Free from Compulsive Eating,* wrote of eating chocolate chip cookies for an entire year. Others ate only peanut butter for months and months. Still others eat french fries, chips, and popcorn for dinner every night for weeks. Your body will eventually want salads, carrots, protein, and fruits. Listen to what your body wants.
2. Ask yourself: "Do I want salty foods right now? Crispy foods? Doughy foods? Soft? Sugary? What would most satisfy this hunger?" Again, don't despair if you don't always want "good" foods. Who says you should only have eggs for breakfast, sandwiches for lunch, and roast beef for dinner? For that matter, throw away the concept of eating certain foods at certain times altogether.
3. As often as possible give yourself *exactly* what you want. You may not be able to give yourself an authentic Philly Cheese Steak if you live in Texas, but you can come pretty close if you are truly committed to giving yourself what your body is asking for.
4. Start carrying a "food bag." This idea is found in Hirschmann and Munter's book *Overcoming Overeating*. It is very helpful to have with you at all times snacks that you like and can eat whenever you feel hungry. This cuts down on the cycle of bingeing. You won't get too hungry and slam down any old thing if you have your favorite foods with you.
5. When you have whatever you want in the way of food, let yourself eat. When you're ready, start to tune into the feeling of fullness.

WHEN YOU ARE FULL

For a long time I was able to eat when I was hungry, and pretty much eat what my body wanted. But stopping when I was full took a whole new level of trusting and listening. I realized how much I depended on food to do so many different things for me. It was not just my physical hungers I had been feeding all these years, but my emotional and spiritual hungers as well.

—Marie

Our bodies come equipped with a natural signal that tells us when we are no longer hungry. A baby turns from her mother's breast. An animal simply stops eating. Their bodies relay the information to their brains that they are full and that's it. Simple, natural . . . and extremely hard to do for a person who has listened to everyone except herself about how much she should eat.

Stopping when full may be the most difficult behavior to learn. It really takes a lot of slowing down and going within to our very guts to hear or feel that natural stop signal. Every person's signal is different. For some the signal might be that they lose interest in what they're eating. For others, it's a physical sensation; for still others it's a "knowing." The signal is there, it just might take a while to recognize it fully. Be patient with yourself.

Another reason why this signal might be hard to get in touch with is because when you don't know when you are hungry, you are not going to know when you're full. If you eat something that is not truly satisfying, you won't feel satisfied. It is a process that starts and ends with information that comes from within. The more you follow your own bodily directions the quicker you will learn a very new-old way of eating.

Stopping When You Are Full

1. If you have waited until you are hungry and you have eaten exactly what you wanted, let yourself stop eating as soon as you are full. For some people, this is indeed a challenging assignment. Your fullness "regulator" might be on the blink after years and years of dieting and bingeing. Don't worry, the signal is still there and you will eventually hear it if you listen closely.

2. Try to eat without distraction for a while so that you can hear the subtle cues of fullness. Try to tune in to your body and your food as you eat. Feel your body being nourished by this wonderful substance. Eat slowly and gratefully. You are performing the holy act of breaking bread with yourself. Bless the food as it goes into your body and think about all the wonderful people who made it possible that you have this food to eat. Think about the abundant earth and nature, which are the original source of all nutrients. Thank yourself for giving yourself nourishment.
3. When you have had enough, ask yourself these questions:
   a. "Am I satisfied?" If the answer is no, find out what else you need. If the answer is yes, then listen to the answer and stop eating. Remember that when you eat past fullness, it will be impossible to hear another fullness signal. What comes next is only the feeling of "too full," and that can be very uncomfortable.
   b. "Do I want more? What else do I want?" If you are not sure, wait awhile and ask again in a few moments. Sometimes it takes time to feel fullness after eating. Remind yourself that you can always have more as soon as you are hungry, even if it's only a few minutes later.
   c. "Can I stop now?" This is the hard question. Many people feel an incredible sadness when they are no longer hungry. Especially if they are used to eating a lot more than they seem to be eating now. If you have been in the diet-binge cycle for long, you are used to eating very little food, followed by eating lots of food. If you are anorexic, you are used to self-starvation and your natural appetite is well hidden. You can learn to stop eating when your stomach tells you to stop, not when your head tells you. For everyone, it will take patience and time to get your own natural appetite back.

Some people take years to really get this part of the program down. People who have the most problems are the one's who try to rush through these steps or turn this into the eat-when-you're-hungry-eat-what-your-body-wants-and-stop-when-you're-full" diet. This is not a diet! There is nothing to "go off." You cannot fail this part. There are only eating experiences, and some are easier than others. When you lovingly nourish yourself, and work on the issues that drive you to overeat, you will find that eating becomes one of the most pleasurable experiences you can have. Like a baby who knows its hunger, knows what it wants, and turns its head away when its full, you too will again get in touch with this natural appetite. You will have a sense of peace you never thought possible with food.

TRANSFORMING OUR RELATIONSHIP WITH OUR BODIES

Myths are tales that are told to help understand life. They bypass the analytical mind and speak to our hearts. The following myth has been written in order to explore from a distance how our relationship to our bodies has changed from a loving, respectful one to a distrustful and even abusive one. As you read through it, think of Gaia as representing the inherent wisdom of your earthly body, and Rhiannon as representing the part of you that is still searching for your true identity.

In the clearing on top of the hill lies the sacred circle of stones, standing tall and still, as if waiting in silence for the dance to begin. If you sit next to them, you can feel the pulse of the earth coming up through your feet, beating strong and steady. As you lift your face to the sky you can feel the sunbeams gently caressing your face and you can hear the whistling winds of heaven. There is a moment, a magical moment when the day turns to dusk, that if you look very closely with your eyes and with your soul, you can catch a glimpse of Gaia and Rhiannon. You can see their bodies swaying and moving with the pulse of the earth. As they dance in the sacred circle of stones, their naked bodies shake and tremble with the greatness of life and abundance of pleasure. Sparks of all colors fly from their feet as they hit the ground, turning into long wisps of light that dance around them. Gaia and Rhiannon dance together to celebrate their sacredness, to birth their creations, and to honor all life.

There was a time long ago when they stopped dancing together. And this is the story I shall tell.

Gaia was a beautiful goddess. She was born of the deep, iridescent, magical darkness where all sacredness is created. Because of Gaia's ability to be a vessel, a container for creation, she became the mother of Rhiannon, another goddess who carried the qualities of the bright, starry skies where dreams are birthed and sacredness is celebrated. As the mother of Rhiannon, Gaia's passion was to keep Rhiannon alive and vibrant, to help her to experience their world fully, and to help Rhiannon manifest her dreams. Rhiannon respected Gaia's magical powers and flourished with them. She honored Gaia by valuing her wisdom and seeking her guidance on her path through life. Together they celebrated their journey, their sacredness, and the sacredness of their world. They danced with light, and they danced with truth, and usually they danced for hours. Their adventures, together in their world, were full, joyous, and many.

One day Rhiannon decided to explore other worlds. On her expeditions she heard many wonderful songs and stories that were different from any she had heard before. They were stories about great, powerful gods that held and controlled the wisdom and truth of their world: truths entwined with conditions, truths to be celebrated upon attainment . . . they were not the given truths Rhiannon was accustomed to.

She was fascinated by the different ways of these worlds and listened attentively to these stories, all the while vowing to explore further. But few of the stories acknowledged the existence of Rhian-

non and Gaia's world. And when they did mention Rhiannon and Gaia's world, the stories were told in a way that made her world seem wrong and shameful. The stories colored all she had celebrated all her life with a darkness she had never known. The more she listened, the more uncomfortable and frightened she became. Rhiannon stopped celebrating her sacredness. She tried desperately to hide her amazing gift of creativity from the other worlds and their storytellers. She banished her dreams. The magical power of her dance with Gaia was gone. She stopped dancing. Rhiannon was very embarrassed about her world and especially about Gaia. She began wishing Gaia was like the gods and cursed her for not being more godlike.

Even though Gaia could see what was happening and tried to remind Rhiannon about her own unique beauty, Rhiannon would not listen to her. And if by chance she did hear something Gaia was trying to tell her she didn't believe it because she had forgotten about Gaia's sacred wisdom and distrusted her. Rhiannon resented Gaia so much for not being more godlike that she tried to force her to change through various cruel methods. When Gaia would not easily change Rhiannon thought she was out of control and needed to be locked up and disciplined. She took Gaia out of their lovely world and locked her up in the other world, feeding her only the tiniest morsels to survive on. When Gaia would not and could not become a god, Rhiannon became more angry and resentful and began berating Gaia, calling her names and telling her how ugly and useless she was.

Throughout Gaia never lost her connection to the great, iridescent darkness where all sacredness is created. She never, ever forgot who she was. Gaia tried to yell out and scream to Rhiannon to listen to her and to remember. She cajoled and pleaded with Rhiannon. She rebelled and raised havoc. She even tried to please Rhiannon. She did everything she could to get Rhiannon's attention—but Rhiannon was blinded, too busy trying to be something she was not. Gaia never gave up. She continued to try to get Rhi-

annon's attention, and at the same time did everything she could to protect herself from the shame and abuse that she received from Rhiannon and the other worlds.

Gaia and Rhiannon died hundreds of lives together with Rhiannon never hearing or fully seeing Gaia. It was very, very sad.

One day Rhiannon was bringing Gaia a vessel of water and she knelt over the vessel to bless it just as she always did when she was feeling sorry for Gaia. Who knows what it was that day—maybe it was the rainbow that was coming through the prison window that danced around the edges of the vessel, or maybe it was some magic web that had been woven by the gods and goddesses above and below. But for some reason, Rhiannon caught her reflection in the water and saw a sparkle of light dancing in her own eyes. It triggered a memory—a memory of long ago. She closed her eyes and remembered a long, long time ago when she and Gaia would dance and dance, and as they danced they would see these sparkles of light dancing within and around themselves. Slowly Rhiannon opened her eyes and looked at Gaia and remembered.

She remembered all of the beauty and wisdom that Gaia held. She remembered the miraculous ways in which Gaia had kept her alive and vibrant. She remembered how Gaia had taught her to experience the world. And she remembered how Gaia had supported her in manifesting her dreams. And she saw reflected in Gaia's eyes her own love and sacredness. She grabbed Gaia's hands and they danced together with joy, and they kept dancing throughout all of the worlds.

—Carol

Like Rhiannon, women have died hundreds of lives without ever remembering their own sacredness. And like Rhiannon, women once knew and valued the beauty and wisdom of our bodies, represented by the goddess Gaia in the story above. When we look closely at the way most women relate to their own bodies, we find tragic, misguided, and distrustful relationships. Like Gaia, our bodies have been given the miraculous job of experiencing the physical world and manifesting our dreams. Yet as women we've learned to ignore our bodies, distrust them, and cut off all communications with them. We cannot see our own unique beauty and wisdom; instead, like Rhiannon, we have been taught that our bodies are wrong and shameful and we try to force our bodies to become something that they are not, through various tortuous methods. And our bodies, like Gaia, do everything they can to get our attention and at the same time protect themselves.

But it hasn't always been this way. There was a time when women's bodies were not treated like objects but were honored for their spiritual properties—the miraculous ability to give birth and nurture new life. But over time this connection has been lost and repressed through the rise of the patriarchal culture that defined spirituality in masculine terms. Goddess images with all different body types have been found: for example, the earth mother of Laussel with huge breasts and belly honoring the sacred female, the vegetation goddess with small breasts and large thighs and buttocks representing the fertility of the earth, the goddess of Mesopotamia who offers her breasts as a sacred gesture honoring the milk of life, and the tall, thin bird-faced goddess with her arms raised high, bringing the life-giving energy of the sun to the earth. Women's images weren't created for the purpose of selling beer, new cars, and other products. Nor were they intended to be a commodity to control or manipulate in order to get what we need or define our self-worth. We were goddesses—to be honored and respected as sacred. *SACRED. Our bodies are sacred.* Try that—say it to yourself—wear it—"My body is sacred." Sacred means holy, consecrated, and to be revered. It also means to be secure against violence or abuse. We need to take back our original right to have our bodies seen as they are and treated as sacred. But to do that we must first learn to believe it ourselves.

We must know and feel deep in our hearts that our bodies, *exactly as they are,* are to be honored and respected by us. Through our own reverence for our bodies we take the first major step toward securing ourselves against violence and infringement. Violence and infringement means hating, criticizing, forcing starvation (dieting), ignoring our bodily cues of hunger and fullness, forcing our bodies to be something they aren't naturally, and stripping away our bodies' spiritual qualities. We can change our relationship with our bodies from one that always struggles and fights what our bodies are telling us to one that honors and empowers them. We can expand our relationships with our bodies to include the incredible spiritual, emotional, and physical wisdom that we hold in the feminine body. When we can do this we are free to work with our bodies to manifest our dreams, whatever they may be.

JUST THE WAY YOU ARE

I spent so many years fighting and hating my body that it just became a way of life for me. My whole existence focused on trying to lose weight and knowing that I couldn't be in a relationship, get a job, or be happy until I did so. My body was never right; even when it was thinner it was never quite thin enough. And then when it was fatter it was horrifying to me—the grossest thing on earth. So much hatred and disgust I poured onto my body! No wonder it had to get so big. I had to protect myself from myself. When it was suggested that I just accept my body size as it was for now, I panicked. I wondered, "What if I stay fat all my life?" But what was even scarier was how could I ever accept my body size just as it was right now? For most of my life I'd been trying to change my body; to stop that seemed like asking me to become a whole new person. And it was. Because the person I was before was consumed by one goal—losing weight. When I was willing to let that go, and just accept my size for now, for today, I discovered something else: myself.

—Joan

Learning to accept your body *exactly as it is*, right now, in this moment, is one of the most challenging steps in the recovery process. After years and years of hating and loathing your body, blaming everything on your weight, creating fat as your enemy, it is a radical and disturbing thought to switch the rules and begin to make friends, even to forgive and love your worst enemy. But the truth is that your body, every ounce of fat you carry, is not your enemy. It is a part of you, a part that has been shamed in a culture obsessed with thinness. If you are above or below your natural body weight, you need to honor how your body is serving you.

> *When I was an adolescent my father started molesting me. As I grew womanly hips and breasts his obsession with my body grew and the sexual abuse became more elaborate and more frequent. My way of dealing with this unbelievably horrible practice was to say nothing verbally to anyone. Not to my mom, my sisters, my teachers, or my friends. I thought it was my fault for getting "too sexy and grown-up." This is what my father told me and I believed him. My response was to get smaller. To try to go back to being a child. I stopped eating and lost so much weight I had to go to the hospital. Eventually my parents divorced and the truth came out about my father and what he did to my sisters and me. However, it took me a long time to get over my obsession to be thin. I was over twenty years old before I had my first period.*
>
> —*Beverly*

Beverly tried to protect herself by becoming very thin. Since she couldn't control what was happening with her family, she took control of the only thing she could—her body. Sometimes it can appear that exerting power over our bodies is the only way we can enjoy any sense of control in our lives. It seems that this is the only way we can protect ourselves. We let our minds overrule the natural hunger or fullness signals in our body in order to cope with an overwhelming situation. Many times, gaining or losing weight is an unconscious process. We're not really aware of why we are doing it and it can feel as though we're completely out of control, even though there is a very wise part of us taking over. We are rebelling against, or protecting ourselves from, a situation that has brought us pain or which we instinctively know is harmful to us.

Relationships were always hard for me. I always felt like there was something wrong with me, so I always thought people really didn't like me. I felt self-conscious every time I spoke to someone and felt shy in big groups of people. Lots of people I knew who felt like me would drink to get over their fears but I grew up in an alcoholic family and I refused to ever become a drinker. It became easier and easier for me just to stay home and be by myself and eat. At first it was just me that there was something wrong with, but after I got really big it was my weight. I knew I was so huge that no one would want to talk to me. My fat kept me from meeting men, getting jobs, and going to social events, and I hated it. But eventually I realized that I also depended upon it. I was afraid to live my life because I was too scared of not being liked. My overweight body helped me to hide out. What I hated so much because it kept me from living my life, I also needed so much.

—*Tracy*

Our bodies respond to our own stresses. They help us cope by giving us a way out of something that we can't handle. For some women it is a familiar role to be the object of the culture's prejudice against fat because they have experienced a similar painful rejection in their past. It becomes more difficult to shake off the cultural messages if they are reinforcing earlier messages they've gotten as children. To be so rejected encourages them to withdraw and isolate behind a screen of cultural hatred that is very painful. It is important to see that many times the body is responding to a core issue that needs to be healed. It will truly be a miracle for Tracy eventually to say to herself, and to the culture, that *no matter what her weight is,* she is worthy and willing to live her life to the fullest.

All my life I was never comfortable saying no. I would do just about anything asked of me. It scared me how often I did things I didn't want to do, especially with men. I felt that I did not have the right to say no. Then I realized that if I was fat then no one would ask me to do anything. This was somewhat unconscious, because I would tell everyone that I did want to be thin and that I did want a boyfriend. But the reality was that I needed to keep the fat on in order to keep people away and to keep me safe from men. I let my body say what my voice could not.

—Rebecca

Our weight talks. Our bodies say what we cannot say. If we have learned that it is too dangerous or too uncomfortable to say what we need to in order to take care of ourselves, then we have to find some other way. Sometimes it is simply that we have no role models of women being assertive and saying no. We think that our only option is to create a boundary with our bodies, and let our bodies make the statement. As in Rebecca's story, it may be difficult to understand what it is our bodies are trying to say. Even so, it is important just to trust that if our bodies are not our natural weight, then there is usually a good reason why. However, many women are already their natural weight but are judged to be "overweight" in our society. These women may not have an eating disorder or any psychological reason for their body size. It may simply be genetics that is determining their size, and their only work is to fully accept their own unique body. Our bodies have an innate intelligence that we all can honor, trust, and listen to. We can stop fighting with our bodies and begin accepting them.

Acceptance does not mean that your body has to stay this size forever. It simply means that in the present moment you make peace with it in order to listen to it and understand it. It means that you completely let go of the goal to change your body size. Your energy and focus is needed elsewhere.

Creating Acceptance

1. Draw an outline of your body, front and back. Don't worry about making it realistic or artistic. Color in the parts that you don't like with one color, and the parts you do like with another color.
2. Label each part and write down next to each one why you do or do not like it.
3. Then go through each part and try to remember where it was you learned to like it or not like it—the cultural or familial negative message you learned about that body part. Write this down next to the body part.
4. Starting in one area, close your eyes and breathe gently and effortlessly as you focus your awareness on this part of your body. Then ask what this body part's gift is to you—what it does for you. Write this down next to that part. Close your eyes again and breathe with focused awareness into that body part and tell that part, "I love and accept you exactly as you are." There may be some body parts you can't say this to yet—that's okay. It's to be expected after years of hating our bodies. If there is a body part you have difficulty with, say, "I am trying to love and accept you exactly as you are." Continue this exercise with each body part.

For particularly difficult body parts see the Communicating with Our Bodies exercise in Chapter 4, page 79.

SELF-ABUSE

When I was eleven my mother took me to the doctor because I was overweight. They put me on a strict diet. I remember sitting at the dinner table with all of my brothers and sisters who got to eat whatever they wanted, and I couldn't. When I wanted more I was told no. When I was hungry in between meals I was told I wasn't hungry. This is when I started to sneak food. Kids at school began to tease me and call me names. At first I was angry at them and hated them all. Then I began to think they were right. I began calling myself those same names. This lasted for years, until finally I went away to college. There was no one to tell me not to eat. I was free to do anything I wanted. But I continued to diet, continued to tell myself I wasn't hungry when I was and that I couldn't eat what I wanted. I continued to deprive myself and call myself names even though no one else did. Here I was, finally in a safe environment, and it was too late. I didn't need anyone outside of me to treat me this way because I had become an expert at doing it myself.

—Beth

To not feed our bodies when we're hungry, to overeat when we're not hungry, to feel shame about our breasts, to hate our stomachs and to say negative things to ourselves in the mirror is self-abuse. Our liberation from this kind of abuse comes as we learn to own it. This healing process begins by noticing how every day we abuse our own bodies and are verbally abusive (in our heads) to other people's bodies we see walking down the street. This is extremely difficult when this culture constantly gives toxic messages that we all internalize. It requires an incredible amount of support from other women who are also in recovery, and are also trying to stop the abusive cycle.

When I started becoming aware of how many times I beat myself up in my head, I couldn't believe it. But even worse was when I tried to stop it! It was so second nature to me that changing it was like trying to learn a new language. It felt alien to me to say nice things to myself. When I would say to myself, "You look gross today!" it felt comfortable—like an old shoe. But then I began to realize that it really didn't feel good to me—it hurt! And it would put me in a terrible mood for the rest of the day. To get in touch with these feelings I had to stand there in front of the mirror and ask "What does it feel like to say this to yourself?" Slowly I began saying "It's okay." Not "You're okay," because that was too uncomfortable. Just "It's okay," like I was talking to a two-year-old. And it felt much better.

—Jocelyn

Most of us don't think twice when we say abusive things to our bodies. Yet when we witness a parent talking to a child in an abusive manner, it makes most of us cringe. It's painful to watch the wave of shame that passes over the child's face as their precious spirit shrinks. When we say abusive things to our bodies, it is just as damaging. There is a part of us (usually our own inner child) that believes it and takes it in and *wears* it. To change this behavior is to take a step closer to knowing our bodies, and therefore ourselves, a little better. It takes us a step closer to the love of ourselves that can truly heal the negative relationships we established with our bodies.

Stopping the Abuse

1. Identify an abusive statement that you make to your body, for example, "That fat on my stomach is gross!"
2. When you find yourself saying this statement, try stopping it. For example, "It is not okay to say that anymore." At first you will catch yourself after you've said it. With *lots* of practice you will be able to stop it while you are saying it.
3. Replace it with a neutral or positive statement. A neutral statement might be, "There is fat on my stomach." A positive statement might be, "The fat on my stomach is fine exactly as it is," or if you're really willing to risk it, try, "I love the fat on my stomach."

If it is too uncomfortable to say the positive statement to yourself, then stick with the neutral one for a while until it gets easier. Then move on to a more positive statement. It is all right if it feels very awkward at first. It should—it's new and completely opposite to what we've all learned. There's an old saying that many people find helpful: "If you don't feel awkward doing something new, you're not doing something new." Eventually your positive statements will not only feel more comfortable but more truthful.

OBJECTIFICATION OF OUR BODIES

What I learned about being a woman was that I should be tall and thin with large breasts and sleek thighs. I learned that women's bodies were to be used to sell cars, perfume, clothes, computers, alcohol, cigarettes, and just about anything else. I learned that as a woman I was supposed to always be on a diet, and there were a million products out there to help me. I learned that as a woman I was supposed to wear control-top panty hose to keep my stomach from sticking out, high heels to make me taller, and push-up bras to make my breasts look larger. I learned that I was to agonize over what I was going to wear that day. I was supposed to be completely obsessed about my looks but never let anyone see me look at myself or else I would be vain. I learned as a woman that my body was an object to be molded into something that it was not. I don't know why I wasn't taught that my body was not an object to be twisted into something it could never be. I don't know why I wasn't taught that my body was sacred and deserved honor and respect. I don't know why I wasn't taught to look in the mirror and see my Self. I often wonder how my life would have been different if women's bodies were not treated as objects.

—Carol

By de-objectifying our bodies we can see that we are more than an object to be used. Our bodies are interconnected with our minds and spirits. Once we see ourselves as whole (and much more than our "fat thighs") we can see others as whole beings as well.

I remember so clearly my mom dressing me up, putting bows in my hair, and pushing me out in front of all of her friends. "We want to show them how pretty you are," she'd say. After they'd gone she'd tell me everything they had said about how cute I was. I learned to live for these comments. I was like a dog learning to do tricks for a treat—only for me it wasn't a treat. It was my mainstay. I was so starving emotionally that I lived on strokes—first from my mother's friends, then from my friends, and then my lovers. To this day when I get dressed I have to remind myself that I am not just my looks—there's a bright, loving child in there and I can see her now.

—Colleen

Although this may seem like an extreme example to some women, many of us have learned that being a woman means playing the role of living for comments or strokes by others. Hearing comments by others about our bodies or weight has become just as familiar as hearing comments on the weather. The problem is that we learn to base our self-esteem on what other people say about our bodies. Some women have learned to cope with this cultural intrusion by keeping themselves up to the cultural standards so they can never fall from grace. Like Colleen, many women spend an incredible amount of time, energy, and money trying to "perfect" their bodies so they match cultural standards. However, they eventually fall from grace because at least one part of their bodies is either "in" or "out" every ten years. That's just how it works. Women learn to depend upon the opinion of everyone but themselves to define their worth. We aren't taught that our bodies are perfect just exactly as they are. We aren't taught that we aren't just our bodies but are very beautiful spiritual and emotional beings. It took Colleen years to be able to finally see her "Self" in the mirror because she was so conditioned to look at her "appearance." We spend so much time and energy playing the role we've learned as women, obsessing about our fat grams, weight, and looks, that we can't evolve past that role into the one that is rightfully ours: becoming very powerful, creative beings. Living in a culture that is obsessed by looks and weight represses the rest of our wonderful dimensions.

De-Objectifying Your Body

Experiment looking at your body and other people's bodies as if there is a spiritual being inhabiting them.

1. When you catch a glimpse of yourself in the window, instead of noticing how you look, try saying "Hi!" to yourself. Try to actually see your Self in the mirror, instead of just measuring your body.
2. When you look at a model in a magazine, instead of obsessing about how thin she is and how you wish you looked like that, try thinking about the actual person in the picture. Try asking yourself, "I wonder what she likes to do on Sunday mornings?" Or "I wonder how she feels about herself. What are the things she worries about? What are her hopes and dreams? What was she like as a little girl?" When you are walking down the street and find yourself judging someone's body, try asking, "I wonder who she is as a person?" You are trying to move away from the one-dimensional view of her body size and expanding your perspective to include room for the whole being.
3. When you are looking at your round stomach (or some other body part you dislike) in the mirror, instead of sucking it in, say, "What a great belly you are! Thanks for all of the things you do for me!" This moves you away from just noticing it as an object and moves you toward acknowledging all of the other properties it contains.

Continue to observe how many times you find yourself or others treating the body as an object. See how your perceptions can change when you are willing to let go of judgments about yourself and others. It's amazing how quickly the universe can expand in dimension when you expand your own vision of it.

COMMUNICATING WITH OUR BODIES

> *"The language you speak is made up of words that are killing you."*
>
> —MONIQUE WITTIG, *Les Guerillères*

Most women's communications with their bodies are limited to negative, critical comments. Once we learn to stop these, or at least slow them down, we create room for more positive interactions with our bodies. We find that women who actually engage in positive dialogue with their bodies or parts of their bodies shift their focus from the body to the person. There are many different ways of talking with our bodies and it's important to find one that's comfortable for you. Some women find that just listening to the body, identifying where the aches and pains are, where they feel uncomfortable or tight, is beneficial. Some find that speaking to their bodies in soothing and comforting ways is helpful. Sometimes it can be helpful to imagine talking to a specific part of our body that has been particularly difficult to accept.

Learning to Communicate with Your Body

For this exercise it may be helpful to tape record your own voice leading you in this communication. Get into a comfortable position and if you'd like, close your eyes. Bring your awareness to your breath. Notice what it feels like to breathe in through your nose, down into your lungs and belly, and back out again. Use your breath to bring your awareness into your body and away from your busy mind and all of the stresses of the day. Just notice the natural rhythm of your breathing; don't try to change it. Notice the rising and falling of your belly and chest. Scanning from your head all the way down to your toes, notice if you are holding tension in any of these areas, and if so, breathe into the tension. As you breathe out release any tension that you may be holding, allowing your whole body to relax. Let the couch, the floor, or the earth completely support you—there is nothing that you have to hold up. With each breath allow yourself to move deeper into your Self, deeper into that place within you where you hold your wisdom, deeper into your truth.

From this place, get in touch with a particular part of your body you dislike. Just choose one for now. You can do this imagery at another time with a different part if you'd like. Breathe into the part of your body you've chosen. Try to feel this part of your body, both the external form of it and what it feels like on the inside. Let it relax, releasing all of the tension from it. Now try to get a clear picture of this part of your body. You may see it as if you were looking in a mirror, or you may get an abstract picture of it. It doesn't matter—just try to get some image that represents this body part for you. If you can't get an image, that's okay too. You may just feel it. Sometimes it helps to place your hands on this part of your body to help bring your awareness into it.

Imagine that this part of you has a personality all its own—a shape and a name. Let the image of this part of you show itself. Let yourself observe this part of you. It might be helpful to let this part sit across from you at a table or next to you on a bench. Have a sense of openness and wonder about meeting and really getting to know this part of you, just as you would do if you were meeting a new friend for the first time.

Now let this part of you "speak" to you as if it had a voice of its own. This part of the exercise may seem odd to you at first, but stick with it, and have patience.

As you start to get the hang of it, let your body part tell you what it's been like to have you dislike it so much. Let this part of you tell you what it would like you to say instead. It's been here a long time and probably has a lot to say, but it might be scared or too shy to talk right away. *Be patient!* If you stay with it, and keep your sense of wonder, it will eventually speak. The "voice" you hear will come from your "imagination," and that's fine.

Now tell this part what you want. It may not be able to accommodate you, but it and you still need to have all wants and desires out in the open. You may want this body part to be bigger, or smaller. It may want to be loved exactly as it is.

Hear what it says back. See if there is a compromise that would please you both. This is a part of you and so only with the agreement that you can both live with will any change occur. Keep in mind that any agreement you make can be changed in the future. This is a dynamic, growing process.

Once you have reached a stopping place, thank this body part for communicating with you today and thank yourself for the willingness to do this work.

Let yourself come back slowly to reality. Take some deep breaths. Breathe in energy, calmness, and peace. When you're ready open your eyes and remember all that you were shown. Lovingly stroke or pat the part of you that you used to dislike.

From now on, whenever this part and you seem to be in opposition, repeat this exercise to dissolve the hatred.

SEEING YOUR BODY

We have found that mirror work is one of the most challenging yet most powerful ways of seeing and then communicating with our bodies. It is the most challenging because we have spent most of our lives using the mirror as a way to judge our appearance. To change this pattern is very difficult. It means becoming intimate with ourselves. And for those of us who weren't taught how to do this it can be quite uncomfortable and even scary.

Working with a Mirror

This exercise works best if it is done frequently and consistently. We recommend doing it three times a day, but if that is too difficult to fit into your schedule try to do it at least once daily. You will need a full-length mirror that reflects your whole body from the top of your head to your toes. If you don't have one, get one. Put it in a part of your home where you feel safe and comfortable. You might even want to adorn it with flowers, lace, or anything else to help make it into a sacred mirror, one that reflects your uniqueness.

For the first few times, just stand in front of the mirror. You may want to be fully clothed. This is fine. The goal is eventually to be able to stand naked in front of the mirror so that you can see your whole body. Check in with yourself first by looking into your eyes. Say hello to yourself. Notice how you are feeling about doing this and just acknowledge how difficult it may be for you. Then slowly allow yourself to start to look at your body as a work of art. Try to stay on a level of discovery, noticing the different shapes, colors, and textures of your body. For example, you might find yourself saying, "I'm round up here, and straight here. I'm softer in these areas and harder here."

Every time you find yourself criticizing your body or using words that have a negative connotation (like flabby, saggy, etc.) stop, and look back into your eyes. Take a deep breath and let it go. Try to say to yourself, "I love and accept myself exactly as I am." Then try again to go back to that body part and describe it without the negativity.

When it becomes difficult and it feels as though you can't let go of the criticism, or when you start to get tired, notice that, and then let yourself stop the exercise. Look back into your eyes, take a deep breath and let it go, acknowledging the work that you were able to do (even if it's just standing in front of the mirror for a few seconds, because for many of us that in itself is hard to do). Try to close the mirror work by saying to yourself again something like, "I love and accept myself exactly as I am," or "I am learning to love and accept myself exactly as I am." Come back to it another time or another day when you feel fresh again. Sometimes you may only be able to do the mirror work for a minute or so, and that's just fine. You will slowly be able to tolerate more time in front of the mirror as you expand your ability to see your body as it is—not as it is seen through our internalized cultural judgments.

We encourage you to do this until there is no place on your body that holds a strong charge for you. This may take weeks, months, or years. Eventually you will get to the place where you don't need a daily reminder, but you may need a tune-up mirror session before or after stressful situations that might trigger body criticism (class reunions, weddings, bad days, and so on).

BEING IN YOUR BODY

Our culture teaches us to live mostly in our heads, and not in our bodies. Many times we are so lost in our thoughts that we lose the subtle signals that other parts of our bodies are giving us. Some of us have learned, through varying degrees of trauma to our bodies, to dissociate, separating ourselves from uncomfortable feelings in our bodies. Part of this work is learning to be present in our bodies, moving out of the obsessive thinking in our heads and into feeling what is happening in our bodies. This helps us learn to identify our bodily signals of hunger and fullness, and our physical and emotional needs.

Inhabiting Your Body

This exercise was adapted from the exercise "Body Scanning," found in the excellent book *Transforming Body Image: Learning to Love the Body You Have* by Marcia Germaine Hutchinson. It is a way of bringing your awareness into your body.

1. Lie down on the floor with your legs uncrossed, arms by your sides. Notice how you are feeling in your body. Begin to pay attention to your breathing, simply noticing how this happens for you. Don't try to change anything, but rather trust that, after all these years, your breath knows how to breathe itself. Just allow yourself to breathe naturally and notice . . .

   - what parts of your body move when you breathe?
   - in what order are they moving?
   - are you breathing through your mouth or through your nose?
   - are you inhaling all the way, or is there some restriction that prevents you from taking a full in-breath?
   - when you exhale, do you empty your lungs completely?
   - follow your breath and use it as a means to getting to know the inner areas of your body.

2. Try to sense how much of the surface of your body is present in your awareness. Scan your surface to discover which areas of your body's surface are clear and which are vague or missing entirely from your awareness.
3. Bring your attention now to the way that your body is lying on the floor. How are you feeling on the floor? Light? Heavy? Free? Constricted?
4. One by one, breathe awareness into each body part. Starting with your head, take a deep breath in, bringing your breath and awareness into your head, and as you breathe out release any tightness

or tension you may be holding. Continue on with the rest of your body, breathing into your neck, shoulders, arms and hands, upper and lower back, chest, solar plexus, belly, pelvis, buttocks, thighs, calves, and feet.

5. Now scan your body to discover where you store emotions. To locate an emotion it is often helpful to imagine a situation where you felt that emotion and then to notice where in your body you experience that feeling.

    - Where in your body does your anger reside?
    - Where in your body does your love reside?
    - Where in your body does your guilt reside?
    - Where in your body does your shame reside?
    - Where in your body does your fear reside?
    - Where in your body does your mother reside?
    - Where in your body does your father reside?
    - Where in your body does your joy reside?
    - Where in your body does your wisdom reside?
    - Where in your body does your power reside?

6. Now experience your body as an integrated whole. Say to yourself the following, inserting your own name: "This is my body. This is where I, __________, live." Take a deep breath and say it again. Feel the impact of these words on you. Take a minute and write down any thoughts or feelings that came up for you during this exercise.

(Reprinted with permission from *Transforming Body Image: Learning to Love the Body You Have* by Marcia Hutchinson, Ed.D © 1985. Published by The Crossing Press: Freedom, CA.)

TRUST

In our culture we have learned to mistrust our bodies and to view them as something we need to control and manipulate. We have also learned to discount the wisdom of our bodies and listen *only* to the external advice we are receiving from others. When we stop viewing our bodies as uncooperative and out of control we can begin seeing them as very wise teachers. Our bodies are living intelligences—they usually give us immediate feedback about what does and doesn't work for us. When we start to trust them as such we can understand what it is they really need, beyond a certain number of calories or fat grams.

Trusting Your Body

Take a full day to trust your body completely to tell you what it needs. It's usually best to do this on a day when you don't have anything else planned, so that you can be spontaneous. Trust your body to tell you if you're hot or cold, hungry or full, tired or active. Listen to its signals. If there's an ache or pain, try to figure out what your body needs to ease the pain; then take the time to do it. Follow whatever messages you are getting. If you are tired, allow yourself to sleep, rest, or even just close your eyes for a moment. If you are hungry, let yourself eat. If you don't feel like talking, allow yourself to be quiet. If you're feeling a certain way—angry, happy, etc.—trust it and know there's probably a good reason why, even if you don't know what it is. Devote the whole day to listening to your body, trusting its messages, and responding to what it needs. At the end of the day take some time to record your experience—what was different about this day and what you discovered. Write down some ways in which you trusted your body that you would like to try regularly. Although it may seem impossible to do this on a typical day, you can start by incorporating small steps in trusting your body on a daily basis.

NURTURE

It's so important to provide some time and space in our lives to nurture our bodies in ways that we want to. Going to the gym to work out because we have to in order to lose weight is different than going to the gym because it's something that feels good to our bodies and is pleasurable to us. When women in our groups get in touch with what they really want to do to nurture their bodies it is usually something quite different than what they thought they should do. Whether it's going for a walk, getting a massage, taking a bath, lying down, making love, saying no, or staring into space, you will know if it is right for you if it is pleasurable to your body.

Nurturing Your Body

1. List ten things that you believe you *should* do for your body
2. List ten ways of nurturing your body that you *want* to do
3. Try at least five of the ways that you *want* to nurture your body and see if it feels pleasurable. If not, knock it off the list and try another one.

SEX, WOMEN, SHAME, AND GUILT

When we begin to live from within outward, in touch with the power of the erotic within ourselves, then we begin to be responsible to ourselves in the deepest sense. For as we recognize our deepest feelings, we begin to give up, of necessity, being satisfied with suffering and self-negation, and the numbness which so often seems like the only alternative in our society.

—Audre Lorde, *Sister Outsider*

When I started to get in touch with the real reason that I hated my body so much, the feelings of deep-seated, through-and-through shame about my body was the feeling that came up the most. Following it back to my adolescence, I remembered at that time my older brother started teasing me about starting to grow breasts. Before that age I was welcomed in my brother's baseball games, but as soon as I started looking too much like a girl, I was no longer able to play with the guys. My mother started to treat me differently, as well, by keeping a closer eye on me. My father withdrew from me and wouldn't hug or kiss me as much as he always had. Boys and men started to yell remarks at me as I walked down the street. I lost my individual identity, my freedom, and my enjoyment of my body. I started to hate the way my body looked and the only thing that made me feel better was to stop eating. I was starving myself, but at least I got rid of my breasts and thighs.

—Susanne

In our workshops and support groups, participants frequently share stories about the feelings they have concerning their sexuality. Invariably the stories they share bring up emotions that range from deep compassion to horror and grief. We find that two emotions, shame and guilt, are predominant, making women feel that they are not good enough to enjoy sex, leaving them utterly numb to their sexual feelings. At the opposite end of the spectrum, the same feelings have made many women more sexual than they wanted to be in particular situations. In order to be loved, they felt they must be perfect. In order to be loved, they felt they had to "put out." Both of these ideas stem from the relentless feelings of shame and guilt about what it is to be feminine. Somehow we have gotten the idea that a good girl should not enjoy sex, her body, or her sensual feelings. The cultural pressures to be "superwomen," and to look beautiful while doing it, creates women who are not only afraid of their own sexuality but many times they are actually repulsed by sex. How can a woman relax and enjoy intimate relationships while she is holding her stomach in? How can a woman enjoy sensual pleasure with her mate if she is constantly worried about her cellulite? How many times does a woman go to bed and have sex simply because it was expected of her? And if she said no, would she ever be asked again, especially if she thinks she is overweight, old, ugly, or somehow not "sexy"?

How often do women simply stop eating because they don't want to have hips or thighs—the very parts that make us women? How many women starve themselves in order to look unwomanly and thus asexual? How often do women throw up their suppers because they do not want their lovers to see their fat stomachs when they get into bed? How often do women put weight on to insulate themselves from sexual attention, attraction, feelings? How often do women keep weight on in order to make themselves unattractive to the opposite sex, so that they will "stay out of trouble," or so that they won't be wounded again? These self-monitoring devices help women protect themselves. In some cultures women cover themselves head to foot in order to save men from their own presumably uncontrollable lusts. What is the difference between covering themselves in cloth or covering themselves in fat or revealing they are nothing but bones? All are ways of disappearing, of hiding.

Not many men share these feelings with women. Although men feel the pressures to be ready for sex at a moment's notice, to be tall, muscular, "hung," and to have a full head of hair, men generally let themselves enjoy sex more than the average woman does.

> *The religion I was raised in was very much male dominated. Starting with the very first story that I remember being told, I knew that my being a female was a very bad thing. It appeared that once upon a time, humans lived in a paradise. But then after God made a woman from a man's rib, things got really screwed up. Eve* made *Adam eat an apple. We were kicked out of paradise immediately. Over food!!!! And we had to endure a very painful way of giving birth. The nuns I lived with could do everything at the school except the holy ritual of saying mass. For that we had to have a male priest from the school down the street come to our school, and, even though*

there were plenty of eager and willing girls ready to serve, we could not. We couldn't even become altar boys! Well, this convinced me that I did not want to be a little girl that would grow up to be an evil woman, hungry, and in pain. I prayed to an all-powerful male God, "Please, make me into a boy." I promised to be "good" the rest of my life if He would do that. It didn't work, so I tried my best to not ever be hungry and to be as skinny as possible. I was already starting my anorexic tendencies at about age six.

—Laurelee

We can trace back thousands of years to see where women got the idea that their bodies were somehow wrong, dirty, or actually dangerous. There are biblical references made to the "unclean, dangerous woman." Women have been blamed for wars, for crop failure, and for driving men to rape and pillage. There are still women today who feel dirty when they are menstruating. Go back to a not-so-distant history of the witch hunts in Europe and America to see how dangerous women were perceived to be by our forefathers. It is not known exactly how many women were tortured and then murdered by hanging, burning, or drowning, but estimates range into the millions. The naming of women as witches and hags continues to do us harm. There are still cultures today that perform mutilation of the female sex organs in order to stop women's natural sex drive. In countries all over the world little girls are valued as sex objects first and are bought and sold as sex slaves or child brides. According to the Rape Crisis Center a woman is raped every one and a half minutes somewhere within the borders of the United States. These practices create shame, terror, self-disgust, fear, and depression in the hearts of women, and a deep-seated belief that her sexuality does not belong solely to her.

In the society that we live in today we honor women who are young, slim, and beautiful. What happens to a woman's self-esteem and sense of self-worth if she does not think that she is young enough, slim enough, or beautiful enough? She starts to look for solutions. For many woman, plastic surgery, dieting, and makeup are all answers to the quest for perfection. How often would a woman put herself through surgery, deprivation, and the cost of makeup if the world cherished a woman's natural beauty and sexuality at any size or age?

> *I still could not get the idea that my female body was sacred for a very long time. I worked hard on accepting it, loving it, and trusting it. But my wide hips, my round belly, and size 38 D cup breasts still made me feel ashamed and unattractive. Even though I looked like my mother and her mother before her, they never felt that their bodies were sacred. Finally, one day I was reading a book about the ancient Goddesses. The Venus of Willendorf, the Goddess Inanna, the Goddess Diana. These images were found in ruins dating back to 25,000 B.C. These were images of the divine female, the very essence of the mystery of life itself. All parts of her were blessed and fashioned into shapes of fullness and abundance. From that day forward I started to take back my feminine form and sexuality.*
>
> —*Nina*

Most of us learn about sexuality through a variety of sources—TV, newspapers, novels, movies, family, friends, and experiences. Unfortunately, especially for women, most of these mediums link our sexuality to our body types: we are desirable and sexy if we are tall, thin, with big breasts and pouty lips. We are taught that it is important to be good in bed in order to please our partner but we're not supposed to be "slutty," nor are we encouraged to have our own needs met in the bedroom. And many of the images we see that mirror our sexuality are abusive and violent. The more recent popular models are not only emaciated, they are usually posed in provocative yet passive and childlike poses. Millions of women's books are sold every year that portray women as powerless victims of sexual violence. Yet we as women continue to buy these novels and pay to see movies that reinforce this image. It is no wonder that many women feel self-conscious and uncomfortable in our bodies while having sex. We have taken these cultural messages and carried them in our bodies as fear, shame, guilt, and powerlessness.

There are many cultures that provide empowering rituals for girls entering puberty, teaching them the sacredness and beauty of their blossoming sexuality. These cultural rituals give their young women an internal knowing and appreciation for this quality within them so when they step into sexual experiences they have something within themselves to hold on to, to protect, and to guide them in taking care of themselves while they are also meeting their own sexual needs. Yet in our culture we hear story after story of women who had sexual experiences in which they weren't able to get what they needed emotionally, physically, or spiritually from their partner and were very wounded in the process. Add to this the notion that her very body is bad and wrong, and it is easy to understand where we got the idea that a sexual woman is doomed.

Sex is a very vulnerable, intimate experience when we are in our bodies and consciously aware of what we are feeling. As women, we are built to open and allow ourselves to be penetrated for sexual pleasure if we so choose. We not only open our bodies but we also open our hearts and our souls in the process. And we do so with the trust that what we receive will be respectful and loving of us, mirroring to us our own beauty and sacredness. And when it's not that way, we usually blame our own bodies. Bodies can experience sexual pleasure no matter what size. It is not our size that limits our experience, it is shame and fear—the same feelings that so often are at the core of our eating disorders.

In our groups, as we are trying to teach women to not only accept but actually love their bodies the way they are, we find that sexual shame and negative body image are two great barriers. It takes a tremendous amount of courage, trust, and hard work to face those barriers, break through them, and walk against the tide of misogyny. When we can go back and reclaim our sexuality for ourselves as the pure, precious, and honorable force it is, we can no longer allow anyone to treat us poorly. We accomplish this as all great things are accomplished—one step at a time.

Releasing Shame and Guilt

1. Start by looking at your body and sexual desires as precious and special. Simply begin by holding this concept in your mind, by slowly allowing it to replace any ideas you might have to the contrary.
2. Start looking at your body through the eyes of love. Become your own lover. Look into the mirror and say to yourself, "I love my whole body. I love my breasts. I love my thighs. I love my belly. I love my butt. I love myself." Give yourself permission to enjoy your naked body by yourself or with your lover no matter what it looks like.
3. Instead of being aware of the surface of your body during sex, i.e., how you look or how you feel to another person (flabby, wrinkled, squishy), go into your body and get into your sensual feelings about your body, i.e., excited, passionate, turned on, or climactic. You may want to check in with yourself in the mirror or do a quick meditation beforehand. Let yourself become child-like and be absolutely delighted with your body.
4. Question any desires to change your body through cosmetic surgery in order to look younger, thinner, perkier, or flatter. Question your dislikes of the changes that come with age.
5. Explore where you learned to feel shame and guilt about your feminine body and about women's feminine bodies. Work on letting go of these feelings.

Every time I get on a scale and judge myself by a pound gained or lost, I lose a piece of my integrity. Every time I diet and don't listen to the needs of my body, I deprive myself of my own truth and my internal wisdom to choose what is best for me. Every time I look in the mirror and see that my body is fat and ugly, I lose a piece of my soul. Every time I judge another person for having a certain body type, I lose a piece of my humanity. And every time I look at my children with critical eyes, I plant another seed of shame.

Hidden behind all of this self-hatred, obsession with imperfection, and trying to be what we are not, is a rich, powerful source of creativity, passion, and power that is the most brilliant manifestation of who we really are in all of our beauty, integrity, and glory.

—Carol

Our relationships with food, our body size, and our sexuality are all woven together around issues of our femininity. It's not just a matter of making our bodies conform to a specific set of cultural standards. It's not just about letting go of unwanted behavior around food. Rather it's about taking back our basic rights as women: our right to feed ourselves when we're hungry, our right to eat whatever we want, and our right to treat our bodies as sacred. These may seem like simple, fundamental rights, but they lay the foundation for our life's work. Who are we in the world if we can't even trust ourselves to know what we want to eat? Who are we in the world if we can't respect our own bodies enough to protect them from self-harm? Who are we in the world if we are constantly obsessing about fat grams, calories, and the size of our breasts, bellies, or thighs?

When we learn to trust our own internal wisdom with food, then this ability transfers to all other areas of our lives. We begin honoring our internal voice. We learn to make decisions for ourselves, not based upon what other people think, but on our inner wisdom. When we hold our bodies as sacred and tolerate less self-abuse, then we hold everyone else's body as sacred and begin to create a world that is safe. When we stop putting our energy into what we're eating or what we look like, we free up this energy to put into other, more creative endeavors. We become very different people in the world. We step out of this destructive cycle that keeps us on a circular path going nowhere, and we step into our own creative power, which gives us the ability to manifest our dreams.

Chapter 5

EMBRACING THE EMOTIONAL BODY

Teach my unskilled mind to sing the feelings of my heart.
—ANNA YOUNG SMITH, "AN ODE TO GRATITUDE," *Women Poets in Pre-Revolutionary America*

When I was overeating, I ate for many reasons. I ate because I was sad, I ate because I was angry, I ate because I was happy, I ate because I was bored. I ate because I was fat. I ate because I was skinny. I ate because I was terrified of being fat again. I ate in reaction to the pressures put on me by the society that had objectified me and reduced me to only a body, without feelings, wants, and desires. I ate because I was anxious or fearful. I ate because I could not feel my own feelings. I ate because I felt like it. I ate because I didn't know what else to do. I had no skills to be able to take care of myself and my feelings other than to eat over them. I was terrified of being overwhelmed by them, by being "eaten up" by them. I had spent most of my life running from them and I did not know how to stop running.

—Laurelee

When women are in the throes of their eating disorders they try many different ways to get well. Most of these approaches overlook the emotional component of eating disorders. So they go through many years of short-term recoveries with higher and higher rates of relapse. Whole groups of foods are taken away and judged "bad" or "addictive" and are therefore "forbidden." Women are taught to weigh and measure every bite of food they put in their mouths. They attend many "weight management" meetings or other types of groups where they sit around and talk only about food, food, food. These remedies are worse than the disease, because they mainly focus on the symptoms, not the underlying causes! Women have told us that they leave these places that are supposed to help them and run straight to the bakery on the way home. It isn't until they stop trying to control their food and weight, start addressing their emotional body, and then learn how to cope with feelings that they find the real cure.

We live in a culture that does not promote *the understanding of feelings;* instead our culture encourages us to put on a happy face, buck up, raise ourselves up by our bootstraps, and shine, shine, shine! How many times do we hear the advice of well-meaning friends and family members who say, "Don't feel bad, don't cry, it will be okay. Get over it and try to look on the bright side." When women with eating disorders are in pain or sadness or boredom, most of the time over- or undereating helps them say these things to themselves. Overeating soothes them, calms them down, and helps them get over their feelings. Undereating makes them feel in control, which in turn calms them down. Carol Munter and Jane Hirschmann, in their wonderful book *Overcoming Overeating,* state that they do not believe that compulsive eaters have an eating problem, they believe that compulsive eaters have a "calming problem." Over- or undereating becomes a tool to calm down, to stop the pain, or to get out of feelings.

I didn't think of myself as having a weight problem until I was pregnant with my daughter. I was home alone and my husband was away a lot. When my security was taken away, food became my friend. I'd had all these networks supporting me before—my weight problems didn't start for me until I lost my network of friends. Food became a tranquilizer—constant and predictable.

—Annie

Like Annie, many women turn to food for solace, support, and security. Often they have used food as a coping mechanism from childhood. It is familiar and it works temporarily, but it comes with a price—denial of feelings robs women of their souls. Sooner or later feelings will surface and they must then be recognized and acknowledged. The same is true of women who stop eating and then become anorexic. For them the denial of their physical hunger and the obsession of controlling their food lets them also deny any emotional hunger. By controlling their food, anorexics are able to feel safe and secure. This keeps all feelings at bay. But, without feelings, you are not really living. As they say, if we don't know pain, we can't really know joy.

Once when my therapist asked me how I felt, I answered that I felt "fat." She surprised me by saying that fat was not a feeling. However, it was the only feeling I knew. Even when I was not overweight, I still felt "fat." All feelings made me feel uncomfortable in my body, so I put them on *my body and labled them "fat." It was a long time later that I realized that anger, sadness, delight, apprehension, joy, despair, etc., were feelings I had, not descriptions of myself.*

—Laurelee

If children were taught how their anger sometimes signaled that their boundaries were being violated, and if they were taught how to stand up for themselves in healthy and effective ways, would there be as much violence in our society? And would many have learned that they have to stuff down anger with food?

What if children learned that tears, even for males, were healthy responses to feelings of sadness, frustration, joy, and vulnerability? Would there be so much sickness?

Unfortunately, in our culture, most feelings are something to be ashamed of, afraid of, embarrassed about, or simply denied.

So what happens to the feelings if we do not express them? They go underground and then pop out in different ways: in wars, illness, rape, child abuse, spousal battering, theft, and in a numbed society that is addicted to every kind of substance, object, and behavior that lends itself to this process. If a person is not allowed to have her feelings and not taught how to process them *and* has an eating disorder, she turns to food or to obsessively trying to control her weight in an effort to cope with painful emotions.

> *In my family it was not permitted to be angry or sad. The only emotion that was acceptable was "fine." I was taught from the earliest age that I can remember to say "fine" each time I was asked how I was. Any other response that I had would be cause for punishment or ridicule.*
>
> —*Emily*

We live in a nation where everyone is always supposed to be fine. It is terribly rude not to be fine. After all, what would the neighbors think? This is one of the reasons that eating disorders have reached such epidemic proportions. Behind closed doors young girls can quietly eat or starve themselves to death. Instead of making her life better for her, the American solution most acceptable to her is to change her body shape. Women of all ages find that instead of getting rid of a going-nowhere job or relationship, the more "feminine" thing to do is to get rid of her fat, her wrinkles, or that "unsightly cellulite."

Eventually some women get mad at the way things are in this culture and they fight back. Feminism is a response to being treated as an object, but so is bulimia, anorexia, and compulsive overeating.

While feminism creates a positive outlet for the anger at being treated as an object and fights to change the objectification of women, women with eating disorders often swallow their anger instead of letting it out.

One of the early stages of recovery involves women letting their anger out in effective ways without destructive consequences. We hear over and over again, "If I let myself get mad, I'll never stop screaming!" But you will eventually be able to own your feelings, go through them, and come out the other side. For a long time it might seem that you'll never get over the anger, or the sadness, or the resentment, or even the boredom of being thought of as an object. When you let whatever feelings you have be okay, and then answer your own inner call for full recognition of who you are, and you stop treating *yourself* as an object, the world in which you live will change and mirror back your own growing self-love and acceptance.

Defining Your Emotions

Today let yourself feel whatever you feel. Even if it is not ladylike, politically correct, or even rational. These are your *feelings,* they are not *you.* Don't try to talk yourself out of them or change them. Just let them be. When you experience your feelings you can have a healthy relationship with them. When you have a healthy relationship with your feelings, you also get to have a healthy relationship with food and your body.

When you start to experience an emotion, see if you can identify it as coming from a specific area in your body. Do you feel your emotions in your chest, your belly, your head? Then see if these feeling have a particular name or description. Is it anger, fear, resentment, joy, indifference?

Ask yourself, does this feeling "belong" to someone else? Is it your mother's, your girlfriend's, your husband's, or your children's? Often we feel other people's distress, sadness, frustration, or anger so strongly that we take it on as our own.

What happened to trigger this feeling inside of you? Did someone say or do something that upset you?

Let your feelings sit next to you, like a friend on a park bench, and have a talk with them. Pretend your feelings are in the ocean, or in a lake and just sit and observe them.

As the awareness of the feeling comes to you, take a deep breath and let yourself fill up with your own feeling. As you exhale, let your breath move all the way through you with the feeling.

You may, of course, not know how to get through these feelings. We will explore how to process your feelings later, so don't worry about falling back on old familiar behaviors. In time, if you stay connected with and conscious of yourself, you will discover how to help yourself go through anything without overeating, undereating, or purging.

FEELINGS UNDERLYING OVER- OR UNDEREATING

When I first tried to figure out what I was feeling I would get so frustrated. I would plan on stopping myself and asking myself what was going on but I never got that far. All of a sudden I would be bingeing and the next thing I knew it was over and there was no way I could have figured out what I was feeling. But I learned to start by sitting down after I had binged and then asking myself what was going on. At first I would get no answer. Then I would just feel frustrated and angry with myself for bingeing. I began to get clearer about what I might have been feeling before I picked up the food. Soon—well, actually it was weeks later—I was able to stop myself in the middle of eating and ask. But I usually kept eat-

ing whether or not I got an answer. Slowly, and it seemed very, very slowly, I began to get better at figuring out what was going on with me, until I was finally able to identify it right when I began reaching for the food. For many, many months I kept eating, even if I knew why, because I still had to learn how to take care of myself in some other way. But at least I was beginning to understand the feelings that I was eating over.

—*Carol*

For those of us who haven't been taught how to identify what we're feeling, exploring the underlying feelings may seem like an impossible task. But like any other skill, we can learn how to increase our awareness of our feelings so that eventually it will become second nature. In fact, eating disorders are a wonderful tool for self-discovery because they give us tangible feedback that something is amiss. Whenever we crave food when we're not hungry, or we start thinking our thighs are too fat, or we start wanting to count fat grams, it is usually a signal that we're having some uncomfortable feeling or that we're in some uncomfortable situation. Once we become aware of these signals, we then have the perfect opportunity to look beneath them at the underlying feelings and the original wounding they might be related to. We then learn how to process the feelings in a way that won't be detrimental to our bodies and souls, and can be healing instead. We believe this is a skill that is essential to living a happy and fulfilling life, and it is worth all of the time, commitment, and patience it requires.

Discovering Your Feelings Connected to Over- or Undereating

Set aside a time of day when you usually overeat or undereat and try to be alone or at least have a place to retreat to. When you notice yourself overeating or undereating ask yourself, "What am I feeling right now?" If you get an answer right away, that's great, but don't worry if you don't. It usually takes quite a bit of practice before the answers come quickly or easily. Many times when we are eating we aren't even aware of what we're doing until it's all over. Just as in the example above, you can still explore the feelings you have afterward, and eventually you will be able to do it before you start eating. After you've eaten, ask yourself again, "What am I feeling?" Close your eyes if this helps and take a few deep breaths. Notice how your body feels. Do you feel tension and tightness? Where in your body do you feel these sensations? Is your body tired and/or relieved? If so, where in particular are you feeling these sensations? Is it sore or uncomfortable? Where? Are you experiencing any emotions that you can label (for example, fear, anger, sadness, joy)? Can you see any images in your mind that help you identify what you are feeling? (These can be pictures of anything—whatever you see is worth exploring.) If you have trouble getting any of this information you might want to refer back to the section titled Defining Your Emotions earlier in this chapter (p. 99).

In the beginning, you may identify the top layer of feelings, that is, the feelings you've just experienced with the food. For example, if you have just binged, you may be angry at yourself. Or you may be sad or disappointed that you have done this again. At the same time you may feel calmer. If you've just undereaten and pushed your plate away after eating only a few bites, you may be feeling guilty because you know you're supposed to be eating more, but at the same time you may feel proud of yourself for maintaining control. Or you may be experiencing anger at a family member who's commenting on what you just ate or didn't eat. If you've just thrown up your food, you may be feeling relieved that you've gotten the food out of your system, but at the same time disgusted with yourself for having to resort to throwing up instead of controlling your eating to begin with. (Remember, these are just *some* of the feelings that people experience. Your experience may be very different and that's okay. What's important is to find your own unique feelings that come up.)

The beginning of this process may just be exploring what types of feelings come up around your behavior. Take some time to write these down. Many times these feelings, when not expressed or processed, can cause us to go right back into the same, or different but equally destructive, behavior. For example, someone who has just binged and purged might binge again because they're so angry with themselves for purging. Or someone who just ate very little and became angry at their family member for commenting on it might go out and exercise for an hour to dispel the anger. We will explore later how to process these feelings, but for now just try to get to know them. Ask yourself what kind of self-judgments come up about your behavior afterward. Do you have these feelings about yourself in other areas of your life? What areas specifically? What kinds of feelings come up that might explain how this behavior helps you? For example, being calm after overeating suggests that you might have been feeling anxiety before you ate. Being proud after controlling your food suggests there may be some shame or fear about being out of control. Being relieved after throwing up suggests there might be fear and anxiety about holding that much food in your body. It's different for everyone, so find out what is true for you.

As you practice exploring your feelings and what may have triggered them, you will notice yourself being able to stop in the middle of the behavior. Eventually you will be able to stop right *before* it. But this may take time, so have patience. This part of the process is extremely important for full recovery, and many times is the most challenging because you have to be completely present with yourself. If you have trouble identifying what you were feeling before you started the behavior, and you've tried the Defining Your Emotions exercise, try reviewing the day's events and see if you can identify anything that might have brought up some feelings, either negative or positive. You can do this by thinking about it or you can actually visualize yourself walking through your day. Maybe what triggered your feelings was a comment your co-worker made that caused you to feel insecure. Maybe it was the positive feelings that your lover expressed to you that made you feel so joyful. Maybe it was just that time when you were home alone and you didn't know what to do with yourself.

Sometimes you can't figure out what triggered your behavior or feelings but you just know there is a blah, gray feeling there. That's okay. You have still identified the feeling and described it and you often can still figure out what you need. Practice as often as you can and you'll find yourself becoming aware of what types of feelings are coming up. Keep a journal if that works for you. Or just write down three-word descriptions (these could be as vague as "gray, ugly, and thick") of what you are feeling. Keep practicing feeling your feelings before, during, and after your overeating, undereating, and/or purging.

FEELINGS UNDERLYING THE FAT THINKING

I can remember clearly the day that Laurelee and I had our picture taken for the Newsweek *article. I showed up at her house feeling so nervous. But the amazing thing was that all morning long I had been thinking about how fat I was! I hadn't thought like that in years. In fact, part of me was sort of shocked, and the other part of me was ashamed. How could I, after all these years of work, still be obsessing about my body? I knew that the best thing for me to do was to tell Laurelee about it, so I gathered up my courage and mentioned it to her. The wonderful thing was that she had been having the same thoughts. We sat down and looked at all of the feelings we were having about these pictures being taken for the article. I was so scared that it wasn't going to turn out well, that I wasn't going to say the right things, that now a million people across America would know about my eating disorder and would see my picture.*

The fat thinking had nothing to do with my body—it was all about my fear and insecurities from the article.

—*Carol*

Fat thinking is the kind of thinking we're doing when we are calling our bodies or parts of them too fat, too ugly, too saggy, too big, or too little. Many times fat thinking is a response to an earlier experience that brought up a feeling that we didn't know how to handle, so we changed it into a fat thought. It is a common process for most people to take feelings that they can't handle consciously and channel them into some other direction that is more comfortable for them, such as blaming someone else. As women, however, because of the cultural messages we've received, we tend to blame everything on our bodies. Hirschmann and Munter in their book, *When Women Stop Hating Their Bodies,* call these negative thoughts about the body "bad body thoughts," and suggest that they "are the way you collude in female body-bashing."

When you begin to understand that much of your fat thinking is not really about your body, then you can start to identify what it really is about, take the blame off your body, and process the deeper feelings in far more constructive and fulfilling ways.

Feelings Connected to Your Fat Thinking

Pick a time when you are having strong recurring fat thoughts coming up for you. It might be before a party while you're getting dressed, in the middle of a conversation with someone, or after you've come home from work, shopping, or whatever. It doesn't matter what the situation is as long as the thoughts are there. You can reflect on the last time you had fat thoughts if you are not currently experiencing them. Take a minute and sit or lie down. After you gain experience with this you can do it anywhere. Close your eyes and take some deep relaxing breaths, bringing your awareness into yourself and your body.

Start by identifying the exact fat thoughts you were having. Then try to see if any feelings you are having are connected to these thoughts. Scan your body for physical sensations as we have done in previous exercises. Try to get in touch with any current feelings there. What might have triggered this feeling? Is this a familiar feeling? Do you remember feeling this as a child?

Now try to completely own the feeling, even if you don't know exactly what it is. Let it be yours, and let it be okay. Tell your body it doesn't have to take on this feeling because you are now able to see it, feel it, and own it. Just acknowledge what you are feeling and assure yourself that it is all right to have this feeling. Later on we will talk more about how to deal with this feeling. But for now, just try to identify it. If you'd like, go ahead and write down descriptions of the feelings.

Repeat this exercise as often as you can, every time you find yourself having fat thoughts. With time it will get easier to identify the underlying feelings and release them from your body.

FEELINGS UNDERLYING THE DIET MENTALITY

I stopped dieting over a year ago. But not a day goes by without some type of diet thought—either counting calories, thinking that I shouldn't be eating something, or wondering if I should go on a crash diet just to lose a few pounds. In the beginning, every time I had an emotional crisis come up I would want to start a diet. Whenever my life felt out of control, whether it was my relationship with my lover or my work, I wanted to go back on a diet. It was as if I was addicted to the dieting itself and I had to go through withdrawal! Eventually I learned that beneath the urge to diet was some feeling that I didn't know how to deal with. So now, a year later, when I think about dieting I know that it's not really the diet I want—it's the distraction from what's really going on.

—Marie

Like fat thinking, the diet mentality can be another response to an earlier feeling that we were uncomfortable with, so we change it into a diet thought. Dieting is a wonderful distraction and obsession because it allows us to focus on something very tangible and concrete, giving us the feeling that we are in control. However, for those of us with eating disorders, it can be just another way to "fix" our problems by looking externally, instead of meeting our own internal needs and ultimately getting much more pleasure out of life.

When we begin to realize that dieting and the diet mentality are symptoms of an obsession that distracts us from an underlying feeling, then we can begin to use the diet thoughts as a way to move into our feelings, into ourselves, and into true recovery.

Identifying Feelings Connected to the Diet Mentality

This exercise is similar to the Fat Thoughts exercise, except it focuses on dieting thoughts.

Pick a time when you are having strong recurring diet thoughts coming up for you. It might be before some event is approaching (like a reunion or wedding), it might be when you're feeling out of control in some particular area of your life, or it might be during a time when you're feeling down and depressed. It doesn't matter what the situation is as long as the thoughts are there. Again, if you are not currently experiencing diet thoughts, reflect on a time you did and use that experience for this exercise. Take a minute and sit or lie down. Close your eyes and take some deep relaxing breaths, bringing your awareness into yourself and your body.

Start by identifying the exact diet thoughts you were having. Then try to see if there are any feelings that you are having connected to these thoughts. Scan your body as we have done in previous exercises and try to get in touch with any current feelings. What might have triggered this feeling? Is it a familiar feeling? Do you remember feeling this feeling as a child? Ask yourself how dieting would make you feel better. See if there's any way in which the dieting or diet thinking helps you to cope with this feeling.

Now try to own completely the feeling or feelings you are having, even if you don't yet know exactly what they are. Let it be yours, and let it be okay. Just acknowledge that this is what you are feeling and that it is all right to have it. Later on we will talk more about how to have this feeling. But for now, just try to identify it. If you'd like, go ahead and write down descriptions of the feelings.

Repeat this exercise as often as you can, every time you find yourself having diet thoughts. With time it will get easier to identify the underlying feelings connected to the diet thinking and therefore releasing the need to diet.

LEARNING TO PROCESS FEELINGS WITHOUT OVEREATING OR UNDEREATING

There is a secret person undamaged in every individual.
—MITSUYE YAMADA

In order to stay with my feelings and not eat over them I had to treat myself as if I were a little child. When I got upset, as soon as possible, I would sit down with myself and just listen to my "upsetness." I wouldn't try to change anything, nor talk myself out of the feelings, I would just "be" with myself. This was almost impossible at first. Sometimes I would sit on the couch for only ten seconds and then I would have to run to the kitchen cabinets for food. Many times I would open the cabinet and just stand in front of it for a moment and then go back to the couch and try again. I must have looked like a crazy woman, going back and forth from the couch in the living room to the kitchen. It was like I was taking myself by the hand and guiding myself through my own tantrum. Gradually, the period of time I was able to stay on the couch with myself got longer and longer. And, when I stayed with myself, there on that couch, the feelings passed and the answers came. Now all I have to do is close my eyes for a second and I will feel the feeling, go through it, and not be overwhelmed. The urge to eat over upsetting feelings has gone.

—Leslie

The relentless urge to eat or to starve yourself when you are upset can seem impossible to overcome. You have to realize that in the moment of overwhelming feelings, you don't know what else to do. *You get overwhelmed with feelings.* You start to drown in them. In a way, overeating or undereating brings you back to yourself, and it then appears that the feelings have passed. The truth is, you have only made yourself numb. There are certainly times when numbing is good enough. But sooner or later it's not enough. You wouldn't be reading this book if it were.

Over- or undereating as a coping mechanism has worked as well as it could, for as long as it could. Now you need to find what else will work. And different things will work for people at different times. When we have learned how to use such a great coping mechanism like food and obsessive thinking about food, it takes aggressive intervention to unlearn it. For the overeater, it takes going within ourselves right when we feel the craving to eat, at the kitchen door, at the door of the bakery, or at the popcorn stand at the movies. It takes going to the cabinet where the cookies are and opening and closing the door thousands of times. For the anorexic it takes letting yourself eat a regular meal even when doing so makes you feel uncomfortable. For the bulimic it takes letting the food stay in your body, being with the feeling of fullness, instead of purging it away. For everyone it takes breathing, and crying, and struggling, and staying there in the moment, asking yourself, "What do I need? What can I do for myself?" It takes throwing eggs at trees outside your deck, like Carol did when she was so mad she needed to throw her anger away. It takes crying your eye makeup right off, putting it back on, and crying it off again. It takes sitting with the boredom of your life and not even being able to obsess about how much better it will be when you are thin. It takes showing up for yourself over and over again. It takes paying attention to what you have been trying to tell yourself forever. It takes telling the truth and taking responsibility for your own truth. It takes letting yourself be angry when you're mad, letting yourself cry when you're sad, sleeping when you are tired, and eating when you're hungry. And it takes letting yourself make the time and the effort to get to know who you are and where you are going. It takes really and truly learning to love yourself—body, mind, and spirit.

> *I was curled up in a ball on the floor. God knows how I got there. I just remember it was all I could do. I sobbed and sobbed and sobbed. I didn't know why. Maybe I was finally feeling all the years of pain around my bingeing and purging. Maybe it was an old childhood wound that I had never expressed. Maybe it was just the fear and loss of not eating like I usually did every time I felt pain. Maybe it was all these reasons and more. It felt like the tears would never stop—but they did. I thought I would never get up off the floor again—but I did. I was exhausted, but I felt better. And I didn't want to eat. This, for me, was a miracle.*
>
> —*Carol*

Who would have ever thought that being doubled over in emotional pain was a miracle? Yet for those of us who have spent years bingeing, purging, or starving, it is a miracle when we can move into our feelings and work through them. Being able to identify our feelings, express them, and then meet our emotional needs is a miracle when we haven't been taught how to do it. Yet it is the key to this recovery.

Sometimes we know we are carrying some difficult feelings around with us but it is too scary to explore them by ourselves. Other times we might try to feel these feelings and we get overwhelmed. Experiencing the feelings may even trigger destructive behavior other than over- or undereating. In these situations it is important to seek the help of a professional who can help you explore your feelings in a safe and nondestructive way.

In order to stop using food or controlling food as a way to avoid uncomfortable or painful feelings, you need to take time to develop compassion for why you needed to escape those feelings in the first place. If you were not taught, early on, to trust and stay with your feelings, if you were never supported in accepting them and going through them, there's no way you could know how.

Staying with Your Feelings

This exercise is designed to help you stay in your feelings and to know you have a right to them. Do not worry if at first you still have to over- or undereat to blot out your feelings, it takes time to learn a new skill. Remember, it is always okay to eat when you need to. Always!

There is a place in your recovery when you have your feelings and you are over- or undereating at the same time. This is part of the process. You will eventually let go of the over- or undereating as you work your way through this program. For now, try to have as many feelings as you can and don't despair over your eating patterns. This is an exercise you can do throughout your recovery. Practice it here by thinking of a time you have had a feeling that distressed you. Reassure yourself by saying over and over, "I am going for the healing. This too shall pass."

1. When you feel a feeling that starts to stress you, sit down as soon as possible and be still. Go to your bed or your favorite chair. If you are not at home, find a quiet spot wherever you can.
2. Close your eyes and let the feeling wash over you. Do not examine it right now. Just let it come and observe what is happening inside you.
3. Stay here as long as you can, without eating, without distraction, without trying to get away.
4. Ask yourself the questions:

    - What am I feeling?
    - What do I want?
    - What can I do for myself to get through this?

5. If possible give yourself what you need. Learn to soothe your own self by giving yourself words of encouragement. You may find that this feeling only needs to be listened to. No action may be wanted. Your own undivided attention is often good enough.
6. If you need to eat, and you know that you are not physically hungry, it is perfectly okay. If you feel that you *must not* eat, even if you are physically hungry, notice that too. Let yourself do exactly what you want to do and at the same time continue to feel your feelings. You may find that you will start eating much less or much more than before even as you are feeling your way through to a greater awareness of your emotions. Be kind and patient with yourself. Patience and kindness are two of the most powerful tools you have for carrying you through the recovery process.
7. Be gentle. You are meeting parts of yourself you've been at war with.

Expressing Your Feelings

If you like, this is a good time to use a tape recorder. It is especially powerful and healing to listen to your own voice leading you on this journey. As with the previous guided imagery exercises, get into a comfortable position and, if you'd like, close your eyes. Bring your awareness to your breath. Notice what it feels like to breathe in through your nose, down into your lungs and belly, and back out again. Use your breath to bring your awareness into your body, away from your busy mind and all the stresses of the day. Just notice the natural rhythm of your breathing, don't try to change it. Notice the rising and falling of your belly and chest. Scanning from your head all the way down to your toes, notice anywhere you are holding tension. Breathe into the tension, filling the tense areas in your body with your breath. As you breathe out release any tension that you may be holding, allowing your whole body to relax. Let the couch, the floor, the earth completely support you—there is nothing that you have to hold up. With each breath, allow yourself to move deeper into that place within you where you hold your wisdom, deeper into your truth.

From this place, get in touch with a feeling. It may be one that you are experiencing right now, or one that you have experienced often in the past and are familiar with. If you have difficulty doing this it may be helpful to find a feeling that you experienced earlier in the week; remember the particular situation that evoked the feeling.

In your mind's eye, picture yourself experiencing that feeling. Visualize what you usually do with this feeling. Do you eat? Do you push the feeling away into the back of your mind? Do you rant and rave over it? Where does it go in your body? Does it get expressed in any indirect way?

Now imagine a very safe space—it could be a room indoors or a sacred space outdoors, whatever is most comfortable for you. This is to be your imaginary art room, a play room. Imagine it filled with every type of your favorite toys and materials . . . paints, water, clay, hammer and nails, punching bags, swings, dolls, writing materials, raw eggs . . . whatever you need to express yourself fully and creatively. Take as much time as you need to create this room for yourself exactly as you'd like it. Now imagine yourself in this room with your feeling. Let the feeling become large and very present. Watch yourself express this feeling in a way that is nondestructive to yourself through some medium in this room. Continue to express the feeling until you no longer feel the need. Look at what you have created. What does it feel like to move it through your body?

Before you open your eyes, look for a way to take what you've done in this room into real life. For example, if you found yourself feeling anger and you threw paint all over your imaginary walls, can you set up an easel at home with a canvas, paper, or cardboard on it and practice splattering paint?

Find a place at home to set aside whatever materials you might need. In the beginning spend some time experimenting with these materials. Experiment with what it's like to express both positive and negative feelings. Once you are comfortable with this, try to do it when you are over- or undereating.

REPARENTING OURSELVES

I believe that this neglected, wounded inner child of the past is the major source of human misery.

—John Bradshaw

During the time that I was trying very hard to stay in my feelings and not eat over them, I had an experience that took me completely back to my childhood. I was sitting and waiting for a friend to show up for a movie date. After about ten minutes of waiting I started to get panicky and very anxious. All that I could think about was eat-

ing and so instead of waiting outside for him, I went into the theater and ordered a large popcorn. When I got to my seat I started to shovel in the popcorn into my mouth as fast as I could. Even though this was usually enough to calm me down immediately, I was still very anxious and uncomfortable. I then decided to close my eyes and see what was really bothering me so much. The image that came was of me as a little girl waiting for my mother to pick me up from school. I didn't know it then, but she had been delayed in a traffic jam that was caused by a wreck on the freeway. School had let out at 2:30 P.M. and by 3:30 P.M. all the teachers and other children were gone. The school was quickly deserted.

As I waited for my mother all kinds of fears and terrors ran through my young body. It was in the winter so evening arrived early. I got more and more panicked as I watched the light fading into dusk. To try to calm myself down, I started playing games with myself like counting the cars coming down the street and saying to myself, "The fifth car will be hers," or "The next blue car that I see will be hers." I also ate all of the lunch that I had saved from before, even though I was not hungry.

When she finally arrived I was almost hysterical and sure that I had been abandoned. That incident, along with other incidents of waiting as a child, stayed with me for so long that every time I was kept waiting, I was thrown back to that very young girl waiting for hours for her mommy, sure that she had been abandoned. This was what was happening in this movie theater. I didn't need food; I needed my mommy to come!

In my childhood, my mother had left me and my siblings at various places, so the issue of abandonment was real, but this particular incident somehow stood out as the worst. I realized in that moment that this was the reason that I always arrived early for every engagement and it was also the reason that I dropped friends if they did not keep to my very narrow time frames. I became abandoned each time someone was late or kept me waiting. It must have been hard to be my friend when no matter what the excuse was, I was near hysteria by the time they did show up.

If I had just eaten myself into numbness, I would have never gotten the chance to go back and heal this very scared and lonely little girl inside of me.

—*Laurelee*

We've found in our own experiences, and in the experiences of women in our groups, that much of the pain underneath our eating disorders is linked to emotional needs that weren't met when we were children. This is understandable since it is impossible for a parent to meet every emotional need a child experiences. However, as adults we can learn to meet our own needs and be our own parents. This is extremely important in recovery, because we use food not only to stuff down our feelings but also to take care of ourselves emotionally (e.g., calming ourselves or controlling situations). When we can take care of ourselves through reparenting, then we can let go of the food. The following exercise will help you identify what your inner child's emotional needs are and how you can meet these needs.

Reparenting Your Inner Child

Once again, get out your tape recorder and find a quiet, safe place to do this exercise. Get comfortable and relaxed. If it is helpful, close your eyes. Think of a time recently when you were very upset. Try to remember the situation clearly, and get in touch with the feelings that came up for you then. Let the feeling be very present and spend some time exploring it. Where is this feeling in your body? How would you describe this feeling? Is it familiar?

See if you can remember a time when you experienced this feeling as a child. If you can't remember a specific time or incident, see if you can picture yourself as a very young person just feeling this feeling. What is the scenario? How are you feeling as a child? How are you coping with this feeling as a child? What are you trying to do as a child to manage the feelings you're having? Is anyone there with you? What are they doing?

Ask this child self you're now in touch with, what she (the child) *really* needs. Just let the answer come. It may come in an image; you may hear it as words, or you may feel it in your body.

Next take a deep breath. See if you can get in touch with the part of yourself that is very loving and compassionate. If this is difficult, you might think of some person or animal that you care very much about and experience these caring feelings that way. Now take this very nurturing and caring part of yourself and picture yourself or feel yourself giving your inner child whatever she needs. Sometimes this is hard at first, but it gets easier each time you try this. If it's difficult to picture this or feel it, try thinking of things to say to her that she needs to hear and then say them out loud.

Notice how it feels to be so loving to yourself. Take some time and reflect on this exercise and if you want to, write down any thoughts or feelings you are having.

What you have just done will help you meet your own emotional needs without using food as a coping mechanism. The challenge is to continue practicing this so that you can learn to do it whenever you are in the middle of feelings that cause you to want to eat or starve or exercise to excess or call yourself fat. You can continue this practice every time you want to overeat or undereat by asking yourself the following questions:

- What do I want to get from either eating or not eating?
- What is my inner child feeling?
- How is she trying to cope with these feelings?
- What does my inner child really need?
- How can I give these to myself?

Do *whatever it takes* to give to yourself what you really need!

UNCOVERING YOUR FEELINGS may be so painful that you feel you can't do it alone. Get whatever help you may need to go through this recovery. Supportive friends, a therapist, or a group is very helpful. But the most important person you need to rely on and to love you unconditionally as you uncover the reasons for your eating disorder is you *yourself.* Be on your own side. Be your own best friend. You have been waiting a long time for you to come home.

Chapter 6

RECLAIMING THE SPIRITUAL SELF

I found god in myself and i loved her/ i loved her fiercely
—NTOZAKE SHANGE, *For Colored Girls Who Have Considered Suicide When the Rainbow Is Enuf*

At first I thought my eating disorder was the enemy—an alien—a disgusting, gross, hateful part of myself that had no purpose except to torment me. But as I look back now I can see that it was the greatest gift I had ever been given because it forced me to look deep within myself, to come home, and to realize that there was something very beautiful and powerful that lay beneath all of the self-hatred and criticism. My enemy was actually my savior—she showed me parts of myself I never knew existed and taught me to love all of myself.

—*Carol*

At the heart of every eating disorder, whether it is compulsive eating, bulimia, or anorexia, there is a cry from the deepest part of our souls that must be heard. It is a cry to awaken, to embrace our whole selves, to see past the limitations we have put on ourselves by defining our bodies or our eating habits as good or bad. It is a cry to deepen our understanding of who we really are. It is a longing to know ourselves in mind, body, and spirit. It is a call from the part of us that holds our desires and passions to grow, heal, and fulfill our dreams. It is a call from the part of us that is connected with a universal love, God, Goddess, great spirit, higher power, a spiritual presence—however you choose to define it—that holds the flame of our true essence of love and light. It is a call from our deepest magic, from the life force itself, to express our true selves.

Like our bodies, in which our innate physical beauty and wisdom has been repressed, our spiritual self has been ignored and invalidated. Our focus in this culture tends to be upon achievement of external, material goals, such as making money, having a nice car, getting good grades at school, being thin, and being "successful" according to society's standards. In our striving for these external goals, we neglect precious inner desires and talents that are waiting to be manifested and expressed.

THE SPIRITUAL SELF

In the silence, I am hearing my own voice again.

—Susan Griffin, *Voices*

God ain't he or she, but a it . . . don't look like anything. It ain't something you can look at apart from anything else, including you. I believe God is everything. Everything that is or ever was or ever will be. And when you can feel that, and be happy to feel that, you've found it.

—Alice Walker, *The Color Purple*

The spiritual self is the part of each one of us that is connected to the wonderful source that created us all. It is the source of the energy, ideas, inspiration, and passion that give our lives meaning and purpose. It is the part of us that feels alive, that animates our bodies. It is what gives us the power to create something out of nothing. When we are fully in touch with our spiritual self we can hear our deepest yearnings and receive our truest guidance.

It is impossible to define a spiritual self that fits everyone's perspective because each and every one of us experiences life differently. We are all unique. Our physical forms are different, the foods we like are different, our talents are different, and we have different concepts of spirituality and what it means to live a fulfilling life. Even people who go to the same church, listen to the same preacher, or follow the same spiritual teachers have different perceptions of their God. It is a very personal, internal vision.

Our spiritual self is connected to the source of creation—the place where all things are united as one, where we all share something in common—call it energy, call it God, call it by whatever name you wish. When we believe we are connected to the source, part of a larger picture, part of that greatest whole, we have a sense of being complete.

Our spiritual self is who we really are. We get so caught up in the physical or emotional self that we forget there is an incredible creative potential that is crying to be expresssed. We are much more than just a body to be sculpted into thinness. We are much more than a little girl wanting everyone to like us. We are powerful, creative individuals who *by birthright* are miraculous, magical beings. We are all part of this source; a source that is neither good nor bad, better or worse, more or less. It is all divine. Every one of us was born with divine spirit. Some of us are just less aware of it than others. When we start to accept this, just as we accept our bodies and our feelings, when we start to open ourselves up to the idea that we came into this world as divine, then we can stop fighting with ourselves and move onto finding out how we want to express our divinity.

When you make enough room for yourself to be divine then you also make more room for others. Instead of needing to critique someone's body, personality, or beliefs you start to see them as they are, expressions of a soul unfolding.

Listen to your spirit—it has a voice crying to be heard. It is different from your body's voice, which has specific physical needs that it is communicating. It is different from your emotional voice, which has feelings that need to be expressed or emotional needs that need to be met. Your spirit has a voice that can guide you, defining your evolution as a spiritual being. It is the voice that moves you with the immense power of your own truth, which mirrors a larger truth that we all share. The voice of spirit moves us not from a needy place, not from a place of physical or emotional hunger, but from a place of quiet and patient knowingness. Be still and listen . . . it is there.

When I was dieting, bingeing, starving, obsessing, I had no other life, much less a spiritual one! I had no god, no angels, no guide, and no inner voice. The only voice I heard was the one that told me how fat I was or the one that kept telling me to eat. In the long road back to my true, inner voice I found that I did indeed have a very strong divine guide underneath all of the yelling, an inner voice that told me that all was well and that I needed to love myself, no matter what. All I needed was to stop long enough to hear it.

—*Laurelee*

Cultures past and present hold many different spiritual truths. Tribal communities live close to the earth and still honor the plants, the animals, the seasons, and the ancestral spirits. Buddhists honor the teaching of the Buddha and believe that through meditation one will hear the truths to live by. Traditional Christianity teaches that Jesus is the son of God and that by having faith in Christ humans will attain salvation and eternal life. Goddess spirituality revolves around rituals of honoring the feminine God and her universe: the moon, the sun, the earth, and the wind, who tell us that the voice is in nature and that to listen to and pray to this will be the only guide we will ever need. Twelve-step programs tell us that in order to recover from a host of addictions we need to believe in a power greater than ourselves, *a God of our understanding*, and the burden of our addiction will be lifted. This is by no means a complete list of religions or religious practices of all humankind, of course. Our point here is that there are many ways of getting in touch with our spiritual self.

Defining our spiritual self is no easy task, especially since we in Western culture are taught that we are mostly a body and a mind. However we are so much more! Our very life is spiritual. We are not humans living a spiritual experience; we are spirits living a human experience. Our soul, our spirit, is as much a part of ourselves as each brain cell, each muscle, each bone. What makes it really hard to define is that we can't see it, smell it, taste it, touch it, or sell it. But, it's there—strong, steady, constant.

Our spiritual body is just as important to take care of as our physical, our emotional, and our mental body. As women with eating disorders, many times we have been at war with each of these parts of ourselves. To call ourselves names and hate our very existence may feel like we are literally "breaking" our own spirit. But spirit can never be truly broken. It is always present, just waiting for us to lift the veils of fear, confusion, anger, and greed, to reclaim our true connection with it.

> *The church I used to go to said that whatever I asked for in prayer, I would get. I would pray and pray to become thin and to be able to eat like other people, but I just got fatter. After being told by my family, and by myself, for so long how fat I was, how out of control I was, and how weak willed I was, I just thought it was my fault for not praying right.*
>
> —*Mary*

How often have we prayed and prayed for someone or something to take this problem from us only to have it still be there? When we look outside ourselves for answers, we sometimes miss or ignore the powerful answers that are within. There is no magic bullet. There is no being "struck thin." To recover from an eating disorder, among other things, often takes a spiritual crisis. The crisis comes when we realize that it is no longer working to look outside for our answers—there is no other way to look but inward.

How do we find this voice of our spirit? Again, there are many ways to do this. Meditation, solitude, song, dancing, prayer, church and chanting are all examples of ways people get in touch with spirit. Again, it is different for everyone and it's important to find a way that works for you.

Spiritual-Being Visualization

We suggest that you read this exercise into a tape recorder so that you can lie down, close your eyes, and just listen without having to read the text. Close your eyes and take a few deep breaths, breathing in total relaxation and breathing out all tension, just allowing your body to ease into relaxation and peace. You may notice waves of relaxation begin to move through you, with each passing moment, with each breath you take, as you sink deeper and deeper into that quiet, still place within you. Deeper and deeper into calmness and peace. Now imagine cords of silver light extending from the base of your spine and feet all the way down into the center of the earth. Imagine waves of relaxation flowing from your feet, through your whole body to your head. Imagine a sphere of healing pink light surrounding you and enfolding you, relaxing you, and protecting you.

Now visualize your favorite place, knowing whatever comes up for you is just fine: there is no right or wrong way to do this. You may see the place, or even just sense the place. It may be by the ocean, in a meadow, in the woods: it may even be inside by a fireplace—wherever you feel secure, safe, peaceful, and centered. Really take some time to create the mood of this place. Feel the texture, smell the smells, hear the sounds, see the colors and shapes surrounding you. Allow this scene to be as vivid as possible.

Let yourself sit or lie down in this special place and imagine a wonderful spiritual being coming toward you. Let yourself take as much time as you need to allow this being to show itself to you. You may want to walk down a path to look for this being. If so, notice what your path looks like. In the next few minutes, allow all the time you need for this being to appear.

What does this being look like? Take in as many details as possible of this being's physical presence. Notice how she/he carries herself/himself. You may see the being, sense the being, or even hear a voice begin to talk. Sometimes the spiritual self appears not as a person but as a presence, an essence, perhaps experienced by you as pure love.

This is the way that your unconscious chooses to show your spiritual self to you. Let however it comes to you be just fine.

Let this being say, do, or communicate something caring, perhaps give you a message to take back with you.

This being knows all about your life. She/he knows what has gone before and she/he knows what is next to come. She/he goes before you to prepare the way. Let yourself really hear, feel, and know what she/he has to say. Let the message sink in to all levels of your entire self. Let it sink deep down into your body. Really let it nurture and comfort you. Rest in the company of your spirit.

This being is always here for you. Always near and close to you. With each new breath, let your heart open up and invite your spiritual being inside, knowing that you will have her or him here for as long as your heart beats.

Take all the time you need in the next few minutes to complete your meeting, saying good-bye in your own unique way. Now allow yourself to return to your special, relaxing place as you continue to remember the nurturing message, knowing that you can bring it back to the room with you. Slowly come back to the room and open your eyes, awake, aware, and refreshed.

Creating a Sacred Space

For so long I had thought that I was depressed and empty inside, that when I first tried to get in touch with my spirituality I found nothing. It helped to surround myself with people, places, and symbols that reflected the spirituality I had inside of me that I couldn't even see yet.

—Barb

Sometimes having an environment that reflects our own spirituality helps to remind us of those spiritual qualities that we tend to forget amid the stresses of daily life. This exercise is to help you create some sacred space in your home environment where you can go and listen to your inner voice, or just mirror back to you your own spirituality.

Start by choosing some part of your living space, no matter how small. It could be a whole room, part of a garden, the top of a dresser, or even a shelf somewhere.

Next, make a list of some qualities that are important spiritual qualities to you. These may just come to you, or you may have to close your eyes and try to picture some things, or you may have to spend some days walking around town or in nature and looking for things that remind you of your spirituality. Once you have this list, try to find ways to represent these qualities in your sacred space. For example, if one of these qualities is openness, you might find an open rose, or a picture of an open palm, or you might just leave an open space in the area. You might choose an image of Christ, Buddha, a Goddess, or whatever expresses your deepest inner beliefs. What's important is that it is yours. It comes from you, expressing your own experience of your connection to spirit. You may watch this space grow and change as your spiritual life grows and changes. Let it evolve as you do.

SPIRITUAL WOUNDS

I believe that in our constant search for security we can never gain any peace of mind until we secure our own soul.

—Margaret Chase Smith

I can clearly remember the day when I no longer believed. I had been going to church school for many years, and my favorite story was still the one of Jesus gathering all of the children around him and saying they were all God's children. Then one day my mother and father separated. On some level I guess I believed it was my fault, because I never again believed that Jesus was talking about me. How could I be God's child when I was so bad that my father had to leave? How could God still love me and take my father away from me? Nothing made sense to me anymore. When my father walked out of my life so did my faith, and it took me a long time to get it back.

—Laurel

Many of us in this culture have experienced some kind of wounding to our spirituality. It may have been a very clear severe trauma, it may have been a more subtle ongoing cultural or familial message, or it might have just been not having any models of people who were actually in touch with their own spirituality. Maybe the real wound is that we feel rejected or abandoned by the world into which we were born. Feeling rejected we try to nurture ourselves—by eating. And the obsession about food and weight only reinforces this separation from our spiritual selves. Healing comes when we recognize our spiritual identity and see that the kind of separation or abandonment we feel is impossible. We can never be separate from spirit. The only separation we can possibly feel is what we create in our own minds. Separation is an illusion, and our healing comes when we address that illusion directly. For those of us with eating disorders, the illusion of separation that we hold in our minds revolves around food and our bodies.

Whatever the case, it can be helpful to take a journey into our past and explore what events took place and what messages we received that taught us to disconnect ourselves from our spiritual self. By doing this we can learn what it was that we needed at the time to encourage our spiritual growth, and we can begin to give that to ourselves now.

Healing the Spiritual Wound

We suggest that you read this visualization into a tape recorder so that you can lie down, close your eyes, and just listen without having to read the text. Get into a comfortable position and if you'd like, close your eyes. Bring your awareness to your breathing. Notice what it feels like to breathe in through your nose, down into your lungs and belly, and back out again. Pay attention to the sensations. Use your breath to bring your awareness into your body, away from your busy mind and all of the stresses of the day. Just notice the natural rhythm of your breathing—don't try to change it. Notice the rising and falling of your belly and chest. Scanning from your head all the way down to your toes, notice if you are holding tension anywhere in your body. Maybe your shoulders are tense, or your belly, or your thighs. Breathe into the tension, imagining that you are sending relaxing oxygen to those areas. As you breathe out release any tension that you may be holding, allowing your whole body to relax. Let the couch, the floor, the earth completely support you. There is nothing that you have to hold up. With each breath allow yourself to move deeper into your Self, deeper into that place within you where you hold your wisdom, deeper into your own truth.

Now try to remember a time when you felt connected to a spiritual source in a positive way. You may come up with a clear image of this source, or it may be a more general feeling of contentment or connection with the universe. You may have to go back very far into your childhood. If you aren't able to remember a time, that's okay too. You can create an image of what it might have been like to feel connected to a spiritual source.

Take a minute to notice what it was like to have a spiritual awareness in your life. How did it make you feel? See if you can get an image of yourself at this time. How old are you? What qualities do you see in yourself that are inspired by this awareness?

Now go back through your conscious memories and see if anything happened to you that cut you off from this spiritual connection. You might remember a very clear, specific incident that happened or it may be a number of small influences. For example, in the story above Laurel can specifically remember that when her parents separated she no longer felt that God still loved her. For another woman, it may be that she became very involved in the pursuit of her career and this specific career didn't nurture her spiritual life. Again, everyone's experiences will be different.

Notice how this affected you at that time. What did you gain from the experience and what did you lose? How did it make you feel?

Now ask yourself what it was that you needed at this time to help you keep in touch with your spirituality. Imagine giving whatever it was that you needed at that time to yourself. Notice how this feels. Now ask yourself what it is that you need *now* to help you nurture your spiritual self. Imagine giving this to yourself. Notice how this feels. Let yourself feel it, fully experiencing whatever it is.

Bring your awareness back to your breathing. Notice how your body is feeling. Notice the sounds and the smells around you. When you feel ready, open your eyes.

Write down your experience and what you needed to help nurture your spiritual self. Try to give this to yourself now in your daily life. You might want to look for a picture or a figure of some kind that symbolizes this experience for you. Keep it in a place that you can reflect on it whenever you wish.

I lost touch with my spiritual self at the moment in my childhood that I realized that I was NOT God. I was female. Man was made in the image of God. I was not man, I was woman.

—Laurelee

MANY YOUNG GIRLS were raised without the image of a female deity. Our saviors were male. Women were either second-class figures (Mary), or shameful (Eve), or victims (saints). As we grew up many girls felt that they did not truly belong in the "divine family of Man." After all, there are no national holidays rejoicing at the birth of a little girl! This exclusive behavior has deeply wounded the feminine.

In order to reclaim our spiritual self we may need to go back to childhood where so many of us were originally wounded. One of the ways to do this is to remember back to all the religious messages that you were given as a child, the positive ones as well as the negative ones.

Assessing Your Spiritual Beliefs

We suggest that you read this exercise into a tape recorder so that you can lie down, close your eyes, and just listen without having to read the text. Get comfortable, close your eyes, and let yourself go back to your early childhood. Try to remember stories, myths, and lessons about religion or spirituality that you grew up with.

As these stories, myths, and lessons come up, write them down. Let yourself do this for as long as needed. In fact, you can repeat this exercise for many days or weeks. That's okay, just keep letting all that you learned and that is deep down inside of you come out.

Once you have a clear picture of your early impressions of spirituality, you will be able to also understand what it is that you still believe.

Go through each of these beliefs and see if they still fit for you. Did any of these messages harm you? Did any of these messages empower you? What in the way of spiritual belief do you still retain today and what beliefs, if any, have you already discarded?

For instance, if you were taught that gods were only males, ask yourself if you still believe this. You might, and that is fine. The difference will be that this is what you choose to believe, not what you are told to believe.

When you have completed this exercise, let yourself sink into your own spirit and rejoice.

SPIRITUALITY, CREATIVITY, AND RECOVERY

> *Nothing is perhaps so wasted in our culture as the energies of its women.*
>
> —Carolyn Heilbrun, *Hamlet's Mother and Other Women*

When I first started trying to get in touch with what I was feeling the only feeling I could come up with was boredom. It seemed like whenever I binged it was right after I would find myself alone, walking around in circles in my apartment with nothing to do. There were many things that I felt I should do—clean the apartment, pay my bills, make some phone calls—but there was nothing that I wanted to do. So I would just find myself going from one room to the other like a lost child—until I finally found the food.

—Marsha

Many women in our groups say they eat because they are bored, but what is boredom? Boredom is either doing something that you aren't really interested in, or doing nothing because you don't know what to do. It may also be a way of avoiding anxiety that's bubbling just beneath the surface. Many of us walk around day in, day out, being bored with our lives. We may be very busy, but there is a low level of boring depression that is nagging at us. It is like a lion in the zoo, pacing back and forth, back and forth, not able to get out of its cage and pursue life as it was meant to be. It's the same with some of us. We pace back and forth in our houses and in our lives, not knowing how to pursue our passions and desires, stuck in old roles that no longer fit our potential. And in order to keep from going mad or from breaking rules, whereby people would call us mad, we overeat, undereat, or obsess about how we eat and what we look like. Fortunately, the difference between us and the lion is that we can learn to let ourselves out of the cage, follow our passion, and choose freedom.

Chronic boredom is a form of depression, and many times depression comes from self-repression, which women have learned to do so well in this culture. We have become accustomed to a cage that represses our own creative instincts. However creation is the food for our spiritual self and celebrates our divinity.

When we begin to understand that our recovery is linked to our need to be our true selves, to find work, play, and relationships that nurture our souls, then we stop waiting for our bodies to change before we take action in anything else. When we realize that we are divine beings *right now*, that we have spiritual needs *right now*, then we can stop waiting until we are thin to participate in our lives more fully. We deserve to live our lives fully right now no matter how fat or thin we are, and it is essential to our healing process that we begin to do so. Finding and expressing our creative passions eventually become more important than controlling our food, losing weight, or looking good. This is true recovery. That's why we say, *it's not about food!* Recovery is not losing or gaining weight by sticking to a food plan and exercise regimen. Recovery is personal and spiritual transformation.

Getting in Touch with Your Creativity

We suggest that you read this exercise into a tape recorder so that you can lie down, close your eyes, and just listen without having to read the text. Once again, find a quiet and safe place to do this imagery and exercise. Get into a comfortable position and, if you'd like, close your eyes. Bring your awareness to your breathing. Notice how it feels to breathe in through your nose, down into your lungs and belly, and back out again. Use your breath to bring your awareness into your body and away from your busy mind filled with all the stresses of the day. Just notice the natural rhythm of your breathing—don't try to change it. Notice the rising and falling of your belly and chest. Scanning from your head all the way down to your toes, notice if you are holding tension in any of these areas, and if so, breathe into the tension. As you breathe out release any tension that you may be holding, allowing your whole body to relax. Let the couch, the floor, the earth completely support you. There is nothing that you have to hold up. With each breath allow yourself to move deeper into your Self, deeper into that place within you where you hold your wisdom, deeper into your own truth.

Try to remember a time when you felt your were in touch with your creativity. It may be a time when you were a child. See if you can picture yourself being creative . . . it doesn't matter with what . . . it could be anything: maybe you are finger painting, or dancing, or making up a play with your friends. Maybe you are swinging on a swing, imagining you're a bird. Maybe you're building with blocks, playing with dolls, or organizing a birthday party. Maybe you even had an imaginary friend. What is important is that you can feel yourself being totally and completely immersed in the process of creating something. If you can't remember such a time, just try to imagine yourself being creative, and notice how old you are. Notice what it is that you are creating. What does it look like? What colors are there? What does it smell like? Notice how involved you are in the process. What are you feeling as you are creating this?

Continue to imagine yourself being creative, watching yourself slowly growing up, and notice if there's any point in time when you began to stifle your creativity. How old are you? What happened? Did someone want you to focus on something else? Was your creativity ignored, invalidated, or just not encouraged? Were you afraid of what you might create? Did your creativity threaten someone or make them uncomfortable? Did you have any role models of adults who were enjoying their own creativity? What messages did you receive about being creative? See if you can pinpoint how you might have learned to ignore your creative desires. You may have a specific memory of something that happened, or you may just have a feeling inside you.

See if there is any way in this situation that you can reparent yourself. Is there anything you need to give or say to your inner child or your adult that received these messages about your creativity? Is there any way you can now, as an adult, give yourself whatever you need to allow yourself to find and express your creative self? What do you need? Imagine yourself giving this to your inner child or adult.

Now visualize yourself as a very creative being. What do you imagine? Imagine yourself as magic, being able to create anything you want. What do you want to create? Let the images flow . . . you may get one or many . . . there is no wrong answer here. What you create could be very practical like a software program, or completely impractical and unrealistic, such as a butterfly that takes people for rides on its back. (Many things that were once unrealistic are now real.) It doesn't matter . . . just trust the images that come.

When you are ready and feel complete, open your eyes and write down whatever it was that you needed to give or say to yourself to help you find and express your creative self. Then write down the images you had of what you wanted to create. Pick one of these images and write down a list of steps it might take for you actually to create this yourself. If you'd like, set aside some time on a weekly basis to work on this project, and let your creativity begin anew!

WHAT IS YOUR SPIRITUAL CALLING?

Throughout my recovery I kept wondering what my true purpose was on this earth. I just couldn't believe that all I was here for was to be fat and then to lose weight.

—Jan

To find our personal calling, we must first believe that we have one, that there is some rhyme or reason for our lives. We believe that we possess a "gift" and that the world would be a better place, and we would be better off, if we found a way to express it. To find our calling is to find the path of our hearts, the way of life that makes us feel alive and glad to be here. Our calling comes in many different packages. For some it is children, marriage, and family. For others it is work that they feel is meaningful. For still others it might be a contemplative life like that of a nun. Our spiritual calling is the path that we were born to be on. When we find that path, we are truly blessed. Joseph Campbell called this "following your bliss."

For women with eating disorders whose lives have been ruled by food and weight, it's hard to believe that there is a greater plan than what they have been living. But there is, and only the individual can find it. When the obsession with food and weight is gone there is a whole new life that opens up to us. When the obsession with vomiting, laxatives, and excessive exercise is gone, we can hear the small voice within. When the obsession with counting calories, fat grams, and weighing and measuring meals is gone, we get to hear what we have been truly saying to ourselves all along. Imagine the time you have spent thinking about food and what you may have accomplished or experienced if that time were directed to spiritual or creative endeavors.

Little did I know that I would lead workshops and groups, write books, and lecture about the very thing that almost killed me. I hated my eating disorder, and I hated myself for having one. But the feeling that remains with me now is one of gratitude. I would have never found out who I was if I hadn't had it.

—Laurelee

Many of the women who come to Beyond Hunger groups just want to stop over- or undereating. Or they just want to change their body. They rarely come because they are wanting to change their whole lives. But in their recovery changes occur on all levels. Women leave abusive relationships. Some marriages become stronger and healthier. Jobs are lost or gained. New businesses are started and new career paths unfold. School is started or stopped. Women move across the country, across town, or just redo their decor. But, no matter what, when you commit to a new path of recovery, things change.

When women start to listen to their inner voices, they also find their outer voices. They start to tell the people in their lives what they need and what they want. They start to own up to what they've always wanted to do, and start to find ways to do it. By following a spiritual path doors fly open and there is nothing left to do but go through them.

How do women stop old patterns of behavior long enough to discover this inner voice? For some, meditation is a very helpful tool. For others, visualization is the tool that works. Still others find that they get in touch with this part of themselves with support from a trusted friend or a therapist.

It seems that it often does take a personal or spiritual crisis to heed our own call. Many people with life-threatening illnesses report that when they learned they were dying, they became very clear about what they were put on this earth to do. Eating disorders are life-threatening illnesses; they hurt our bodies, confuse our minds, and bruise our souls. Going through recovery is sometimes long and hard. And there are no guarantees. We don't know if we'll ever be our natural weight, if we'll ever be "normal" about food, or if we'll ever be happy with ourselves. But to do nothing about the disorder at all is to stay stuck in the pain and helplessness. At some point in time we usually reach a stage where staying stuck is no longer acceptable. It takes courage and love to face what you have to face, and it takes loving yourself, no matter what, every step of the way. And to walk through this process without knowing what lies ahead takes a huge leap in faith.

Getting in Touch with Your Spiritual Path

We suggest that you read this exercise into a tape recorder so that you can lie down, close your eyes, and just listen without having to read the text. Close your eyes and get comfortable. Let yourself sink down into the chair and also sink down into yourself. Breathe deeply and slowly while you let go of the tensions in your body, your mind, and your emotions. Keep breathing.

Go to a place inside where you feel completely safe. Maybe you'll imagine a meadow, a room by the seashore or in the mountains. Set the scene as vividly as possible. See the colors. Smell the sweet scent of the air. Listen to the soothing sounds.

Find a nice spot to sit down in, and image a huge movie screen there before you. Let yourself relax and watch the screen.

Let the image of yourself come up in the present. What is the job you have now? See yourself doing what you normally do all day. Do not get attached to any of it, just let it float across the screen of your consciousness and then fade out.

Let the image of yourself as a little girl come up. What were your hopes and dreams for yourself? Let more images come across the screen. In your childhood dreams were you a mom? a pilot? a doctor? a famous singer or actress? Maybe you saw yourself as all these things and more! Just let your childhood dreams float across the screen and fade out.

Now picture yourself as you are now, but let yourself imagine these childhood hopes and dreams from your adult perspective. Try each one on for size. Imagine yourself in a different role, a role you perhaps dreamed about as a child. Does it fit? Do you really want to be a mom, a pilot, a doctor, a famous singer, or actress? Or something else? You may, of course already be doing what you are happy doing. In that case, just acknowledge what you are now doing with your life and own it completely.

If what you are doing in your life now doesn't make you happy, see if you can let go of it in your mental imagery. Try something else on for size. You don't have to worry about how this will happen; all that's important is to experience how your true calling feels to you. Don't try to change your dream to make it more acceptable, just take what comes.

Let yourself really be in this new role or job or place. Really see it, smell it, hear it, and live it for a few moments.

If one doesn't feel right, try another and then another. Take as long as you need to in order to be very clear about what feels best to you.

When you have found an image or series of images that work for you, let them fade out on your mental screen. Come back into yourself in the present. Let yourself breathe and take it in. Just stay with this for a few deep breaths.

Let yourself come back to the room and take another deep breath and exhale. When you are ready, gently open your eyes, remembering all that you have been shown.

When I started to let go of my obsession with my weight, one of the things I realized was that I was a precious child of God. Toward the end of my recovery I began to see that every step I took along the journey, no matter how strenuous or painful at the time, was also precious.

—Sally

Expressing Your Divinity

We suggest that you read this exercise into a tape recorder so that you can lie down, close your eyes, and just listen without having to read the text. Get comfortable. Close your eyes and take a few deep relaxing breaths, letting go of any tightness or tension. When you feel relaxed, try to get in touch with your divine nature. You may get an image of your divine self, or you may just feel a place in your body that feels divine. Or you may get a word, a sense of light, or a smell that expresses your divine essence. It doesn't matter how it comes. Let the image or the feeling get fuller, brighter, bigger, stronger, louder, until it is very present and tangible for you.

Ask yourself, "How do I want to express this divinity"? Just sit and listen. It may take a long time for the answer to come. It may not come the first time you do this exercise and you may have to do it several times before you get an answer. But keep asking and keep listening. You may get an image, or a feeling, or a saying. But whenever you get a sense of it, try to imagine yourself doing whatever it is. For example if it's expressed through dancing, imagine yourself dancing divinely. If it's expressed through writing, being in relationships with people, flying kites, making love, repairing bicycles, speaking, gardening, or whatever it is, imagine yourself doing it divinely.

The next step is to set aside some time to go practice this expression of your divinity. If you can, do it on a daily basis, even if it is only imagining yourself doing it. You may be able to take five minutes every morning to dance divinely in the kitchen, or garden in your yard, or even imagine in your mind that you are out at the beach flying a kite.

Remember . . . all that comes through you is divine . . . because *you* are.

SPIRITUALITY AND FAITH

When I was in the middle of my bingeing and purging, I felt so alone and so isolated. I couldn't speak truthfully about it because of the shame I had, yet I couldn't stop it by myself. The more I tried to control it the worse it would get. The worse it got the more angry and scared I got, and then I would try to control it even more. It was more than I could handle alone. I used to believe that God was only there for the people who were really good and deserved it, but not for me. So I believed that I had to do everything by myself, without any help. When I slowly began to understand that maybe God loved me, and maybe He had been loving me all along, then I was able to share my burden and ask for help. My faith that He was there for me slowly grew, day by day, and I was able to let go of alot of fear and control knowing that I was not alone. And eventually I learned to trust that whether or not I could see Him or feel Him, He was there, guiding me.

—Brita

When you are in the throes of uncertainty and pain, caught in the destructive cycles of your eating disorders, it is understandable to feel alone, cut off, and unlovable. But if somewhere you can find just a spark of faith in a loving, benevolent source that just might have your highest good in mind, then you can begin to open the cracks in the hard shell around you and let in some light. Faith is trust. When you believe you are connected to a source greater than yourself then you can trust that you are cradled in the loving womb of that source. You can see that each and every event in your life has a gift, a purpose, and you can trust that if you can just find the right perspective you can ultimately gain from it.

If you can trust that you are being held with the greatest love and reverence, wisdom, and respect, then you can let go of your fear and be much more open to the learning available to you through this experience. When you walk through your eating disorder in fear and isolation, trying to control and force your body and mind to do what you want, you miss the process of unfolding. It is the difference between taking a rosebud and prying it open with a knife, and letting a rosebud slowly expand into its full beauty, with the nurturance of the earth and the water and the light. When you open to the nurturance of a spiritual presence in your unfolding, in your healing, then it becomes transformational because of the spiritual relationship that develops along the way. A rose pried open is never as full because it doesn't hold in its heart a relationship with the earth and the light and the water. When you learn to have faith in this process of healing, and learn to trust that there is a loving source of which you are part, then when you heal, you heal with a connection to the source and with others in your hearts.

We once had a friend who was dying of breast cancer who would talk about being in the grace of God. I think what she meant was that when you step out of the struggle of trying to control everything in your life, you allow spirit to grace yourself with the unfolding of your life. In recovery, you sometimes might want to focus so desperately on losing weight, being thin, and stopping certain behaviors that you try to control every behavior in the service of meeting your goal. Having faith doesn't mean giving up responsibility. It means giving up control. Having faith means that when you get to the end of your rope, instead of holding on to it for dear life, you reach out, let go of the old one, and trust there will be a new one. It means you don't have to do it all alone. When you find yourself struggling with something over and over again, you can let it go for the moment and trust that there is a greater source holding it for you. This allows you to rest, not to hold on so tightly, to breathe new life into yourself, to expand and allow for spiritual input and direction. It's very hard to hear your spiritual guidance when you are holding on so tight, driven by your own fear, that you can't breathe and listen.

Expanding Your Faith

Practice this exercise when you feel you are struggling with yourself or your eating disorder:

Stop whatever you are doing, find a place to sit down, and breathe. As you breathe, try for a moment to let go of whatever struggle you are feeling. Ask your spiritual self and your spiritual source to be present with you. Imagine that this source is also holding your struggle for you so that you can let go of it. Then imagine that this source is holding you as you walk through the struggle. Get up and go back to what you were doing, even if it was bingeing, purging, or starving, but do it with the awareness that there is a very loving, caring source present with you. Notice how this feels. Notice what happens as you walk through the same old behavior with a new awareness of this presence. If you'd like, write down any thoughts or insights you have. Continue to do this exercise throughout the week whenever any type of struggle comes up, whether it be with food, with work, or with relationships.

BY RECLAIMING YOUR spiritual self you awaken to your own divinity, which in turn heals the wounds that eating disorders carry: separation from body, mind, and soul. As you begin the process of defining for yourself what your spiritual life needs, you begin a transformation that will take you far beyond the struggle with food and weight. When you look in the mirror and see more than your body, but can actually look in your eyes and see your spiritual self looking back at you, you have begun to transform. When you can get beneath the obsessions in your mind about food and weight and listen to your spiritual voice, you have begun to transform. When you are able to feel positive about yourself not because you are thin, but because you know you are a valuable sacred being, you have begun to transform.

When you look at others with eyes of compassion and respect for their own unique spirit and not with judgment about their body type, you have begun to transform not only your self but your relationship to the world. This is spiritual transformation and this is true recovery.

Chapter 7

LIVING YOUR TRUTH

Truth is the golden chain which links the terrestrial with the celestial, which sets the seal of heaven on the things of this earth, and stamps them with immortality.

—Anna Brownell Jameson, *The Loves of Poets*

For most of my life I had swallowed everything that was fed to me. There were certain beliefs that I took in as a young child and never questioned, so they just naturally became a part of me. At least with peas I was able to hide them in my napkin at the dinner table and then secretly flush them down the toilet. But belief systems are much more subtle. I didn't even know they were a part of me until my early twenties, and then when I began to question them I was really confused. I tried to live within a framework that I had been taught and I lived that way for quite a while. I tried to believe that the most important thing was how I looked or how much I was liked by everybody. I didn't know how to base decisions on what I needed or believed in. But eventually my body and soul rebelled. I could no longer keep those rules down. They were be-

coming toxic to my life's purpose and thus toxic to my soul. I started throwing them up, over and over again because I didn't know how not to eat them. I would just keep taking them in and then just throwing them right back up. Once I learned to find my own truth that was inside of me I could choose between what was right for me and what wasn't. First I learned to do this with food, then I learned to do it with beliefs. Now I'm learning to live it, and let everyone else live theirs.

—*Carol*

Living your truth means actually being able to put into action what your heart and soul desires. Every person has a different truth to tell in their lifetime, each one of us is unique because we have our own calling. However, to find your calling is one thing and actually to express it is another, either because we just don't know how to or because we are afraid to. In recovery it is especially difficult because women have been brought up in a culture that pushes dieting, exploits and objectifies our bodies, and encourages women to please others and be passive. To stop dieting and obssessing about food and weight, to start living our lives and meeting *our own* needs, is to take a radical stance. Never to again say, "Oh, I shouldn't be eating this" or "I'm just trying to lose a few pounds" is never to again engage in a common language with our sisters that we have been speaking all of our lives. To start saying no and instead to express what we really think is to break many of the rules that we have learned growing up.

When we take a new stand or act in a new way, especially a way that is outside the norm, we may experience a backlash or a wave of resistance. It may come from our families, our friends, our colleagues, or even from within ourselves. But wherever it comes from it is usually an expression of fear—our own fear or the fear of those around us. And the deeper the relationship is enmeshed, the stronger the backlash may be. A woman who has put her partner in charge of her food, telling her what she should and shouldn't eat, can expect a strong reaction from her partner when she changes her eating patterns. It will be much stronger than the reaction of a partner who hasn't taken that kind of role in her life.

It is important to find others along the path who understand and can support us in living our truth without the fear and resistance we may encounter as we start to change. While this recovery is a journey, it is *not* a heroine's journey, a martyr's journey, a rescuer's journey, or a savior's journey. Rather it is the journey of the common woman who was born with the intrinsic right to live her truth, whatever that truth may be. There are millions of other women on similar paths as yours, all of them seeking and needing exactly the kind of mutual support that you are seeking in your recovery. You don't have to do it alone!

SETTING LIMITS AND SAYING NO

When I stopped dieting I felt like I was a stranger in a strange land. Everyone I knew was always dieting. For me to take a stand against dieting, especially when I wasn't what anyone would exactly call thin, was a very radical act. And then I realized how often I talked about my weight with my girlfriends and my sister. I couldn't believe it. That's all we talked about! Dieting, diet foods, how fat we were, how fat others were, how much weight we wanted to lose, how much weight others lost, how bad we were if we ate a piece of cake, how thin we once were; on and on and on. It made me sick and I told myself that I was not going to do it anymore. At first, I felt like an outsider. It was as if I wasn't in the "girl club" anymore. We didn't have anything to talk about and I know that they felt uncomfortable, too. It was bad enough that I had refused to go on another diet ever again, but now I wouldn't even talk about their dieting. It took a lot of courage to make that stand, but it was one of the ways I took care of myself, even though it didn't feel like that at the time.

—*Leslie*

When Leslie stopped dieting and stopped talking about dieting, she also had to set limits and not continue to talk about food with her friends and family. She had to make a stand and give up the accepted topic of conversation for women, which made her feel like an outsider. Women grow up hearing their grandmothers talking about weight, their mothers talking about fattening foods, their aunts talking about a new diet, and their girlfriends talking about how much better off they would be if only they could just be thin or thinner. It is the American woman's obsession. This is why we have girls as young as eight years old thinking that they are fat. This is why we have girls as young as ten years old going on diets. This is why we have an epidemic of eating disorders running rampant in high schools and colleges. This is what happens when we have a multibillion-dollar industry whose job it is to scare us with how fat we will be if we don't follow their food plan, buy their diet products, eat their "diet bars," use their exercise machines, or, when all else fails, go on their weighed and measured "shake fast."

> *After I had decided to never weigh myself again, no matter what, I had to visit my doctor for my annual checkup. Before taking me in to the examination room, the nurse stopped in front of the scale and told me to get on. With all the courage I could muster, I told her that I did not weigh myself anymore and I did not want to be weighed now. She looked at me as if I had gone mad, and told me that they had procedures that they had to do. We argued for a minute and finally I told her I would get on as long as I could stand backward and not have to look at the numbers on the scale. She complied and that is what I did. I don't know why she then did what she did, maybe she thought I was in such denial about my weight and that she was helping me, but after I got off the scale, she whispered, under her breath, just loud enough for me to hear,* "A hundred and eighty pounds." *I had to struggle the rest of the day to not "overeat at her."*
>
> —*Emily*

When Emily decided to go against the cultural pressure and not weigh herself, even in the doctor's office, she was setting a limit, not only with herself, but also with the medical establishment! Many like her have felt their self-esteem plummet when they heard themselves measured in pounds. They have sat in doctors' offices and heard all the dieting information they will ever need or have been given some type of supplement or medication, without their physician ever addressing their eating disorder as a whole. They have listened, have taken notes, have vowed to follow the recommended food plan, and have left full of self-loathing, shame, and false hope.

Fortunately over the years we have found many different people in the medical professions who have been extraordinarily supportive of the antidiet movement and who understand the root causes of eating disorders. You can be your doctor's best teacher. Be open and honest about what you have learned about yourself in the process of going through your recovery. Tell her or him about your disorder, what helps and what doesn't. Give your doctor a copy of this book.

> *I knew that I was on the road to recovery when my employer asked for the* millionth *time if I would work late, and I said no. Before then I would have just done it and resented him for asking and been angry at myself for doing it and then I would have eaten my way through the extra work and on into the night after I got home. The funny thing is, while my boss didn't particularly like that I was not willing to give up my personal life for my job anymore, he really didn't give me as hard of a time as I was afraid he would. When I learned to respect my own boundaries about my time, I found that others did too.*
>
> —*Janice*

Saying no to employers, friends, and family members can be difficult. It requires a level of self-esteem that many women don't have but need to learn. In this culture, women have been taught to think of others before they think of themselves. Women are the nurturers, the mothers, the wives, the caregivers. Personally and professionally a women's role is to be of service. But women have not been taught how to nurture and take care of themselves. You don't need to give up being nurturers—moms, wives, caregivers—to take care of yourself. Taking care of yourself is learning to set limits and to say no. Setting limits and saying no does wonders for your self-esteem because it teaches you that you have the right to your own time and your own life.

> *About a year into this recovery, one of the things that happened to me is that I started to lose weight. I was very careful to not get too "tripped up" about it, because I had gone up and down the scale so many times before in my life. So I was trying to take it nice and easy and not project too far into the future as me as a thin woman and all the ramifications about that. However, eventually a few people started to notice how much thinner I was becoming and they started to make comments about it. Before, in my dieting past, when I lost weight, I loved to hear how much weight I had lost and how much better I looked. It validated me and made me feel like I was "good." But, because I was working so hard on accepting and loving myself no matter what, I had stopped ever thinking I was "good" or "bad." So, when people started to comment on my body I found that I had to set limits on what they could say. The phrase that I came up with that helped me the most was, "My weight is not up for discussion." I wanted them to look beyond my weight and see me, the real me that I was letting out.*
>
> —*Laurelee*

As you set limits around "weight talk" with the other people in your circle, keep reminding yourself that in this recovery, weight and how we look on the outside is not the issue. The way you feel *inside* is. Many women go through this recovery and find out that the way their bodies are is just fine and nothing, besides a healthy attitude, needs to be changed. However, some women actually do need to *gain* weight in order to be at their natural body size. Still others will lose weight as they learn how to eat out of physical hunger instead of out of emotional hunger.

The main thing to remember is that the true recovery is so much more than having a body that meets the national style standards. Our bodies come in all different shapes and sizes. A lot depends on our genetic backgrounds, on the stages of our lives, and on our past records with dieting and deprivation.

You will start to learn how to relate to others in ways that don't have anything to do with how thin, fat, short, or tall you are. It takes time to come to terms with the cultural messages we have all been given and taken to heart for so long. It takes even more time to communicate what you have learned to others around you. Especially when so much of the time the rest of the world is still looking at these issues from another level of body awareness.

To really change is to have a whole new way of communicating. You have to open up and be willing to share vulnerable parts of yourself without the protection of standard diet and weight chitchat. You have to want to be seen and you have to want to be heard for who you are, not for how you look. It's not easy to do. It takes intimacy, with yourself and with others. It takes a willingness to be truthful about what your recovery has been about for you—not only about weight but about everything! This recovery is about your whole life.

It is very bold and courageous to say to someone who is commenting on your lost or gained weight, "My weight is not up for discussion." It shows that you are the one who decides how you want others to communicate with you. This is taking care of yourself by setting strong boundaries. It feels strange and somehow not ladylike to set limits, assert and express yourself, and say no to others. But this is how to live in your own truth.

Because I do not work outside the home, I had become very active in volunteering at my daughter's school. I loved my job but because I had so much more free time than the other moms, I found myself doing more than my fair share. Much, much more than my fair share. In fact, I gave so much time to the school that I was unable to take care of my own children when they came home from school. I wanted to learn how to set limits on this, but each time I tried to, I felt guilty and selfish. It took a lot of courage to stop doing so much. As I learned to say no and set limits, I discovered many different truths about myself. While I really loved working at the school and helping out the teachers and kids, much of my self-worth was wrapped up in being seen as a sort of Mother Teresa. I wanted to come across as a selfless servant and somehow that gave me a kind of power over others. I got to be very smug about all that I was doing and would secretly believe that I was better than everybody else. Then, of course, I would bad-mouth the other moms that couldn't do as much as I was doing. Even though I wanted to be at the school and the school was in such need, I had become very unhappy. I was never able to say no or to set any limits around my time or my duties so I felt like I was a martyr and a victim. I had eaten many times over this but until I actually tried to change I never corrected my eating around these issues.

—Tammy

As Tammy started to set limits around her volunteer work she realized all the many reasons she had for getting into this situation in the first place. Her need to be needed gave her self-esteem. Her desire to help was overshadowed by her desire to be loved. As she put her work before herself, she started to get resentful and that in turn made her feel holier-than-thou about the other parents. Her seemingly unselfish devotion to the volunteer position at the school was not only harmful to her but to the others as well. When she learned to set limits on her time, she found that she had to sort through all of the various conflicting reasons for what she was doing. She discovered that she didn't need to be the "super-volunteer" in order to be admired and appreciated. When she let go of the need to do everything herself, others stepped in to do their share as well. She had been keeping a dysfunctional system going because she needed to feel that she was the only one who could do the work. However, that deprived her of her own time and her own family. And when she felt deprived, she would overeat.

She set up a schedule for herself of what she could comfortably commit to and she stuck to it. She stopped worrying about what would happen if others could not step in and gave that job over to the administrators of the school to work out. She was then able to have more of her own free time to herself and to be home when her children came home, which is why she didn't work outside the home in the first place. She learned that the first person she had to set limits with was herself and the rest fell into line after that. When she stopped asking herself to do more than everybody else was doing, nobody else asked her to do more than her share.

Tammy's story is just one example of what the tool of setting limits and saying no can bring up. The important thing to remember is that we get ourselves involved in many situations for many different and (very good) reasons. Some situations are helpful and some are harmful. It takes time and patience to sort through the reasons we are in situations that might be harmful to us and then find solutions for our mistakes. There is a fine line between judging ourselves and then feeling badly, and wanting to take care of ourselves.

Setting Limits

Pick a day this week that you will do nothing that you don't really want to. If you find yourself doing something that doesn't feel good, whether it's overeating, overworking, overspending, overcommitting or just plain doing more than you want to do, notice what comes up for you as you make the decision to stop. Let yourself explore the reasons why you would do something that doesn't feel good. Take time on this day to go slowly. Be gentle on yourself. You are just practicing setting limits. You are just learning how to set boundaries.

When you have an idea of what drives or entices you to cross your own boundary, see if you can get in between yourself and the behavior. Listen carefully to your own self-talk about this. What are you telling yourself? Are you admonishing yourself with shoulds? Or with questions like "What will people say?" Or "What will they do if I don't do it?" Or are you relieved that you don't have to do something you don't want to? Are you happy, even if you are uncomfortable about it? Keep practicing this limit setting and questioning until it feels very natural to take care of yourself by living within your own boundaries.

Saying No

Find a friend or a therapist who will work on this with you. Make sure it is someone who supports you and understands what you are trying to do.

Make a commitment to say no to her once a day for a week. Call her or have her call you and ask you to do something for her. Start with small nos and work up to bigger ones. For example:

"No, I can't go to the movies tonight."

"No, I don't want to type up your homework for you."

"No, I'm not going to able to watch your kids tomorrow afternoon."

"No, I can't make a dozen cupcakes for the bake sale on Saturday."

"No, I don't want to do your laundry."

As you say no this week, pay attention to what comes up for you each time you say it. Do you feel selfish? Guilty? Mean? Bad? Uncaring? Or do you feel relieved? Powerful? Grown-up? In control? Frightened or secure? What? Also notice how often you say no to yourself, and why.

Do you want to give other people all sorts of reasons or excuses why you cannot do this or that? This is unnecessary. A simple no is all that is required.

The second week let your friend start to say no to you. How does it feel to be on the other end of someone setting boundaries? Do you feel resentful or glad that she is telling you honestly what she doesn't want to do? Again, you might feel many different and even conflicting messages coming up for you. Just notice them, acknowledge them, and let them go.

In the third week do not say yes to anything that you really do not want to do. This takes a lot of soul-searching. It also takes really making a commitment to take care of your *whole* self. Maybe you don't want to go to work but you need the money. Negotiate with yourself about the realities of financial truths and then let yourself enjoy your time off when you get it. Eventually, as you keep doing this, you will find that you are doing many more things that you truly want to do. You will have said yes to your deepest desires and no to the things that keep you from them. You will learn that you have a right to say no and when you learn the power of saying no, you will find out how wonderful it is to say yes.

EXPRESSING OURSELVES

> *Wisdom cries aloud in the open air. She raises her voice in public places. She calls at the top of the busy streets, and proclaims at the open gate of the city.*
>
> *Proverbs* 1:20

My husband and I had been married twenty-eight years and had been on every diet there was together. I was the one with the real weight problem however. When I stopped dieting and started bringing forbidden foods into the house he almost had a breakdown.

After all, he had seen me over and over again go on and off diets, and to him it looked like I was on another binge. He kept asking me if I was sure this was the right thing to do, or making comments when I would eat something "bad." I finally had to get up the courage to ask him not to talk about my food at all with me. This was really hard because for so many years this was the way we communicated. . . . It was like trying to find a whole new topic to focus on. At first, I didn't want to talk about any of it with him because I was too scared that maybe I was fooling myself and I was afraid of criticism. Besides—I couldn't even put it into words. But eventually I was able to find the words to express what I was going through, and after some time he could see that my behavior was actually becoming less compulsive. He slowly began to support what I was doing. But it took a while.

—Belinda

Finding the words to explain to our friends and families what we are going through in this recovery may seem almost impossible at first, because many times we ourselves are so unsure of what we are doing! After all those years of dieting and hating our bodies it's a huge shift to start allowing ourselves to eat and be all right with our bodies just the way we are. We may be scared to death that we are going to gain a hundred pounds and become completely out of control, and to hear someone else echo our fears may be too much to handle. In the beginning it can be so overwhelming that we feel all we can do is take care of ourselves—to have to reassure a friend or family member may be too much. But unless you are very isolated, it will most likely be necessary to communicate somehow with friends or family.

Some women find it helpful to give people books to read that explain this approach. Some find it helpful to have their families talk to other people who have already been through recovery. Some have brought their lovers, families, or friends into therapy with them to help them learn about what kinds of support they need and what roles might need to be changed. Some have found that they needed to end relationships that reinforced their own abusive patterns. Some have kept their whole illness and recovery a secret until they felt strong enough to share it.

I had been an active bulimic for five years, and I did everything I could to hide it. When I first came out of denial and realized what was going on, the only person I could talk to was someone who had been through a recovery of her own. And then I found a support system and depended upon the strict anonymity—it was the only way I could feel safe revealing my secret. It wasn't until I was well on the path to recovery that I was able to tell my family. It just felt too vulnerable to tell the people I loved the most.

—*Carol*

Some women have to reach a certain level of recovery before they can verbally express their needs. Other women are able to communicate clearly with their family or friends from day one what they are going through. One way is not better than the other—it is just different for everyone. What is important is to find the best way for you.

I was still living at home when I was at the peak of my anorexia. I had to go to the doctor every three days to be weighed, and what I ate was everybody's business. I understood why they had to do that, but it was so hard when I was trying to learn not to obsess about my weight and not to control everything I put in my mouth. With the help of my therapist I finally got up the courage to tell my doctor that I wanted to be weighed less often because I was trying to stop obsessing about my weight. Just saying that to the doctor was one of the most terrifying things I ever did. And then I decided to tell my parents that I was trying to eat what I wanted, but it was hard to do that when they would focus on every morsel I put in my mouth.

Of course my fear that they would shrink away in horror from the words uttered from my lips was just a fear. And for me it was a huge step because I was able to express what I needed in a new way, without hurting myself.

—Kim

It's natural to be scared when we begin expressing our new needs and feelings to others, especially if we weren't taught to do this. Like any new behavior it feels very awkward and uncomfortable at first. Sometimes we overcompensate in the beginning because we are so nervous, for example by going into a lengthy, intense lecture to some innocent bystander. But as we become more comfortable expressing ourselves we move into a place where we can communicate our truth clearly, cleanly, and powerfully.

The same is true with roles that we have learned to play with our families and friends. When through our recovery we change these roles it may feel very uncomfortable at first and there may be a desire to go back to the old familiar patterns. But with time, and with outside support when neccesary, the new roles become more comfortable and healthier for everyone.

When I was dieting, which was most of my life, I always had someone in charge of my food. It was this person's job to watch me all of the time and make sure I didn't eat what I shouldn't be eating. It began with my mother who sent me to a doctor when I was a child and together they watched everything I ate. Then it became my boyfriends, my husband, and then finally my son. For most of my son's life his main role was to keep me from "falling off the wagon." When I started recovery and I began to eat whatever I wanted he became very upset. After all, I was going out of control and it was his job to control me. It was then that I realized what a tremendous burden I had placed on him and that I needed to fire him from his job. But when I did he was lost. One of his main ways of connecting with me was gone. My therapist had us come in together and helped us create new and healthier ways to be with each other and helped him to finally focus on his own needs.

—*Josie*

As we've stated many times before, recovery changes our lives, not just our bodies and eating habits. And because of this it is bound to affect our relationships. Every different individual who goes through this process experiences a different reaction from their lover, friends, or family members. And it's important to note that they are not all fearful reactions. Many are understanding, loving, and supportive. We just mention the more difficult ones because these are the ones that can sometimes stop us dead in our tracks. And it's at this point where it's important to find help and support from someone who can be understanding, supportive, and loving of you while you are in the midst of this process.

Expressing Yourself

Take a few minutes to breathe and scan your body, releasing any tension or tightness that you find. When you're ready, try to get in touch with something that you feel you need to express to someone. Is there something you've been wanting to say to someone but you haven't been able to? Is there something you want to share with someone but you don't know how to put it into words or are too embarrassed? Take some time to get in touch with what this might be. Don't worry if you don't actually want to talk face-to-face with the person. You don't have to! For now, try to get in touch with what it is you would like to say. Then open your eyes and write it down. Don't worry about editing it now. Just write everything down—all of your thoughts and feelings. When a strong feeling comes up, underline what you were writing and then move on.

When you are done, go back over it and read it again. When you reach the parts that are underlined, try to go into the feeling and fully experience it. Notice how it feels to be experiencing this now, as an adult, and try to imagine or remember a time when you felt it as a child. Ask yourself what your inner child needs, and as you did in the reparenting exercise, try to give this to yourself. Repeat this in each section of your letter where you underlined what you wrote.

Now go back and read it again. If you would like to change it, go ahead. If not, that's fine. Note at the bottom of the page how it felt to express yourself on paper. Leave it for now, and at another time come back to it and read it again. You may feel complete, or you may desire to communicate this in person or through the letter. Or you may not know. That's okay. The most important thing is that you were able to express yourself for yourself. That's a powerful beginning!

FINDING OTHERS ON THE PATH

A vibrant, healthy woman is an unstoppable force for positive change on the planet.

—Carolyn DeMarco, M.D.

I was sure that I was the only one who thought and felt the way I did about food and my body. I felt I could never tell anyone what I was thinking because I believed they would think I was crazy. When I sat with other women who also had eating disorders I was amazed to hear my thoughts coming out of their mouths. And I was so relieved. It was still almost impossible for me to share about myself. I was pretty convinced that they would all gasp in horror at what a mess I was. But when I finally got the courage to speak, what I got was a great deal of understanding and compassion. They knew what I meant! They had been through it also! It was such a burden off my back to know that I wasn't the only one. And it was the first time that I had shown anyone this side of me, and they cared about me anyway. From this I learned to care about myself.

—Toby

Finding other people who are on the same path as you is extremely important in recovery because the changes you make can be very alienating. Taking a stance that is completely against the cultural norm can feel like swimming upstream. It's challenging, tiring, and there will be times when you need to catch your breath and find something to hold on to. There is now enough literature on nondiet programs out there to provide some reassurance. But reading a book is different from connecting with other people because a book can't witness and listen to your process and give you emotional support. It is very important to share parts of yourself and be seen, even in your most desperate moments.

It may be difficult to find others who understand what you are trying to do by stopping dieting, listening to your internal cues of hunger and fullness, eating what feels right to you, and accepting your body exactly as it is. It might also be difficult to find others who understand the emotional and spiritual recovery required to go through this process. But just because it's difficult doesn't mean it's not possible. You may have to look hard. Maybe it's a distant aunt, or someone else's grandmother, or someone you heard speak, or someone you met at a workshop. Maybe it's a friend or lover who is willing to listen because they're your friend or lover. Maybe you have to drag your mother or father with you to a lecture to help them understand. Just keep trying to find someone and stay open to the idea of having a person in your life who can understand and be supportive. If you want to set up a support group, we recommend you read Susie Orbach's book *Fat Is a Feminist Issue II,* where she outlines how to do this.

Living our truth sometimes means being there for *other* people when we're finally ready to do so. When we don't have many examples of self-accepting, nondieting women, we have to create them for ourselves, for our peers, and for our youth. When we are able to live our truth, we model another way. It's not that it has to be the only way. But it gives the rest of the community an alternative model and most importantly a new choice about how to be a woman in this world.

When we find others on the path and we share our experiences we create very intimate and caring relationships, whether they be old or new. This is only one of the many wonderful gifts that can come from recovery.

Chapter 8

TRUSTING YOUR PROCESS

The natural healing force within each one of us is the greatest force in getting well.

—Hippocrates

The lotus flower awaits, patiently, peacefully in the pond, bathed by the sun's rays, caressed by the gentle winds, and nurtured by the water and earth. It seems to be in no hurry, as if it knows that in every moment it is given what it needs to unfold. Each and every petal is tightly curled inward, holding its sleepy bud as if nothing is stirring. But somewhere deep within its consciousness it is in the process of awakening. Inspired by an internal harmony, each petal slowly opens one by one: uniquely, spontaneously, and independently, yet in complete synchronization with each other, falling into place, eager to embrace the day's light. The unfolding is as glorious to behold as the arrival.

—Carol

Like the lotus flower, we are all in the process of awakening. Somewhere deep within our consciousness is the drive to unfold, to express our true nature and be seen so that we can see ourselves. But it is a process—it doesn't happen overnight. The lotus flower has many, many petals that each need to open individually and embrace the light. In our recovery from eating disorders we also have many, many layers of learning that each need to open and receive the lessons. And each of these layers also opens uniquely, spontaneously, and independently.

If we looked at a snapshot of any one person's recovery process, what we might see is this person working on ten different issues, with each issue in a different stage of learning. For example, while Jane may be completely conscious of feeling full, she still may be overeating, and might be very unaware of her constant negative body talk. At the same time Jane may be starting to identify some anger coming up and learning how to process it, but she hasn't yet been able to focus on her spiritual life.

Because there are so many petals to unfold, and every petal unfolds differently from the other, it is impossible to judge our progress by just one petal (for example weight loss or weight gain). As we've stated before, recovery isn't linear. As one lesson gets clearer, another may get fuzzy. One day you may have mastered how to stop eating when you're full, and then something triggers you emotionally, and the next day you are eating way past fullness.

It's important to get comfortable with the idea that it is not helpful to measure your progress the way you used to, which for most women is by the scale. The most common phrase we use in the groups is the best advice we have to offer here: *"Trust your process!"* This means that while there are common experiences for women recovering from eating disorders, each woman works through these experiences and issues at her own pace and in her own way. Once you have opened yourself up to recovery you will find that your intuition and instincts will help you along the path. You can trust that your process is exactly right for you and you don't have to waste time comparing yourself to others. Even when it looks as if you are completely stuck, you can trust that, like the lotus flower, you are unfolding.

THE MOUNTAIN

I have met brave women who are exploring the outer edge of human possibility, with no history to guide them, and with a courage to make themselves vulnerable that I find moving beyond words.

—Gloria Steinem, "Sisterhood," *The First Ms. Reader*

When I was in the midst of bingeing again, for the thousandth time, I couldn't see my way out. I couldn't see behind me or ahead of me. I couldn't see that I had made any progress; it certainly didn't feel like it. I just felt like I had failed again and again and I felt hopeless. It seemed there was no way to get myself out of this hell. I was buried beneath food, self-hatred, fear, and depression. I desperately needed someone to pull me out and set me back on the path one more time.

—Danielle

During the recovery process it is easy to get overwhelmed and hopeless. It's like climbing a mountain in a huge snowstorm; you can't see where you've been or where you are going. For all you know you've been walking around in circles! It's at times like this when it is very helpful to have some kind of marker that can take you out of the whirlwind of confusion and put you back on the path.

We have created a path up the mountainside, one that our groups have found to be extremely helpful. By using this mountain, we don't want you to assume there is a "right way" or a "particular path." It is simply a guideline that we have found is very helpful for women who are in the midst of the process, in the middle of confusion and fear, and need some way of understanding where they are and that there truly *is* a light at the end of the tunnel. The mountain includes both the behavioral changes that we work on and the emotional/spiritual issues that arise along the way. Like any mountain, there are thousands of paths that wind in and out through valleys and hills, woods, and rivers. The work is to find your own path up the mountain. We are trying to let you know where the valleys, hills, woods and rivers lie. How and when you get to them depends upon the path you choose. They may even look different to you than they do to us. What might look like to us a huge, rushing river that feels life-threatening to cross may look like to you a little brook you can just hop over. Don't use our map as your truth. Use it as a guideline to find your own truth. The bottom line is: *Trust your process!*

LETTING GO OF JUDGMENT

The first step in recovery is creating compassion for yourself and your eating disorder. You start this process by exploring how your eating disorder helped you to survive. You learn to let go of the harsh, critical self-judgments you've internalized and begin to develop a nonjudgmental observer that can help you to explore yourself as objectively as possible.

BECOMING CONSCIOUS

As you become more conscious you come out of denial and look straight in the face of your eating disorder. You begin to be aware of how you are overeating, undereating, bingeing and purging, compulsively dieting or exercising. You are coming into awareness of what makes you want to do these things over and over again.

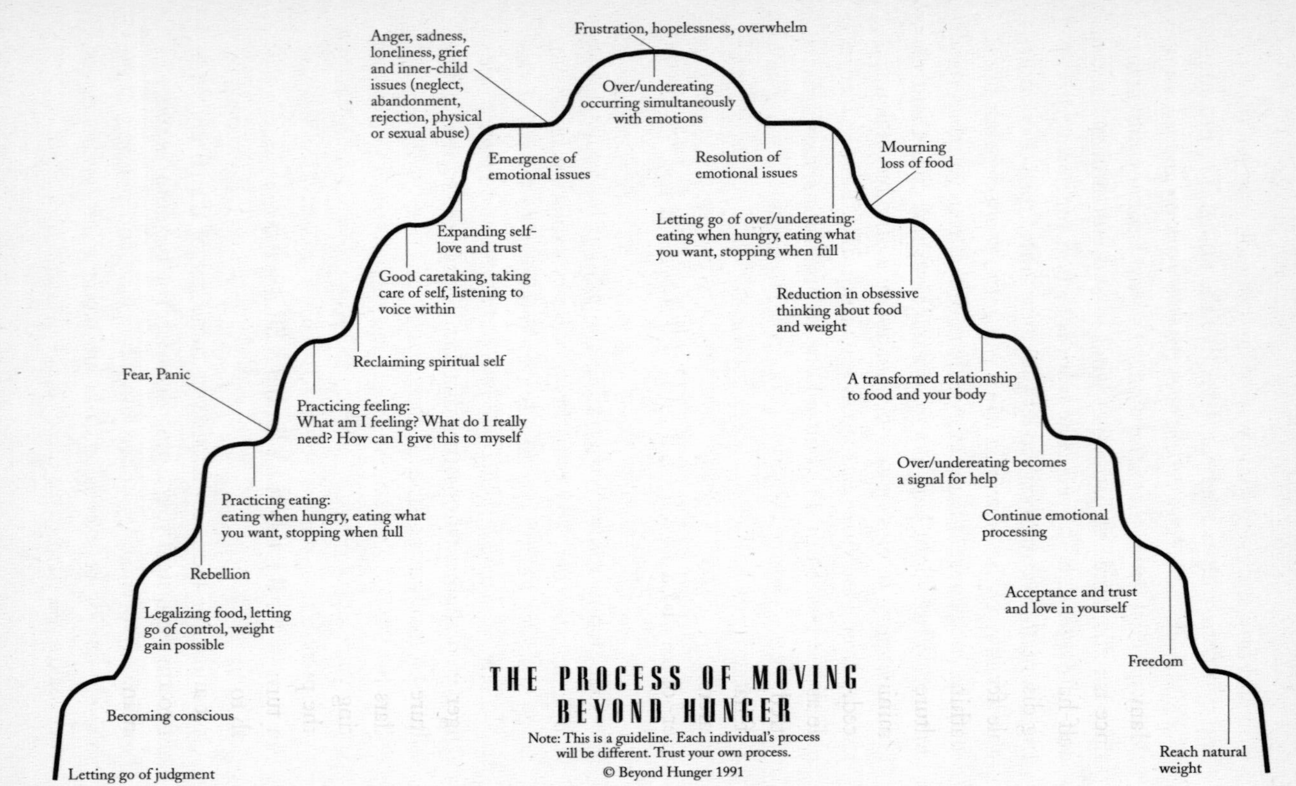

THE PROCESS OF MOVING BEYOND HUNGER

Note: This is a guideline. Each individual's process will be different. Trust your own process.

SELF-HATRED

Many times as you come out of denial, the first emotion you experience is self-hatred for the years spent on your eating disorder and self-hatred for the way you have treated yourself for having an eating disorder. If you allow yourself to stay with this very uncomfortable feeling, and go through it, you will see that self-hatred and loathing of your body has been taught to you. In this misogynist culture we have been led to believe that the female figure and the feminine *itself* is to be changed, made smaller, improved upon, sliced, and diced. The idea that our feminine bodies are not acceptable as they are, and that women are somehow wrong, creates self-hatred deep within the very core of our beings. This much self-hatred can't be tolerated for very long. When you bring your awareness to it, you begin to see why you felt it was necessary to over- or undereat.

ANGER

Anger is at the bottom of these first few processes—anger at the culture you live in, anger at the diet industry that makes millions of dollars by preying on women's fears, anger at your own naïveté for letting your self-esteem get so low. However, you can use this stage of the process to transform the anger that you directed inward; you can turn it outward where it belongs. This transformation is your path to freedom. Anger is a very powerful emotion. By acknowledging it and expressing it constructively, you can use it to bring yourself to the next step in the process of taking back your rights as a woman.

LEGALIZING FOOD AND LETTING GO OF CONTROL

All food is legal. There are no more "good" foods, no more "bad" foods. Ice cream and peas are the same. French fries and chicken are the same. The questions to ask yourself are, "Does it taste good? Do I want it? How do I feel? What do I need? How can I answer my own call?" In order to go through this part of the process, you must let go of control. You don't know yet how you are as an "eater" and you don't know yet how much your natural body is supposed to weigh. At this time some people gain weight, some lose weight, and some stay the same. *It's not about weight! It's not about food!* It is about everything else. You are meeting your true self, without the buffer of food and weight, perhaps for the first time. Everyone is different. Stay with yourself and your process in order to go all the way through the next stage.

REBELLION

During this stage, you begin rebelling from all the years of deprivation—of your food, your body, your self-esteem, yourself. This stage needs to last as long as it needs to last. During this stage you may overeat even more than usual, trying to make up for everything that you have denied yourself for so long. Or you may go through a period of an "I-don't-care attitude." You may refuse to dress "nicely," be a "good girl," or "keep yourself up." You may throw away all the paraphernalia of dieting: books, scales, calorie counters, etc. Believe it or not, these rebellious actions are a very good sign. When you understand that the rebellion is not necessarily about the food you eat or your weight but instead a rebellion against the cultural pressures put onto you as a woman to be perfect, sexy, thin, and young, then you can move away from acting out the rebellion on your body. Stay present, open-minded, conscious, and most important, stay with yourself.

PRACTICING EATING: EATING WHEN HUNGRY, EATING WHAT YOU WANT, STOPPING WHEN FULL

When you eat when you are hungry, eat what you want, stop when you are full, and work on all the reasons that you have an eating disorder, you take care of yourself physically, emotionally, and spiritually. Eventually you will stop the over- or undereating and your body will return to its natural weight. It will take as long as it takes. You cannot rush through any part of this process. Sometimes you will only be able to eat when you're hungry. Sometimes you will have figured out what you *want* to eat but you won't allow yourself to eat it yet. Sometimes you will only be able to eat what you want. And sometimes you will be able to stop when you're full. This is just the practicing part of eating when you're hungry, eating what you want, and stopping when you're full.

FEAR AND PANIC

As you start to eat heretofore forbidden foods, the fear that you will gain a million pounds comes roaring into your life. The panic of not being able to stop once you start will kick in. The terror of "Who will I be if I don't have this problem?" comes up. The fear that you will always be fat, unhappy, and disgusting if you are not at least trying to be on some kind of a diet, is almost paralyzing. This is very scary but completely a necessary part of the process. The way to move through it is to listen to yourself, be with yourself, and learn to calm yourself down. Each time the fear and panic of this process hits, remember: 1) You are not on a diet, 2) it's not about food, and 3) there is always another chance to take care of yourself by eating when you're hungry, eating what you want, and stopping when you're full. Instead of getting stuck in the fear and panic, remember to come back to your center, breathe, and love yourself as you climb to the next level.

PRACTICING FEELING: WHAT AM I FEELING? WHAT DO I REALLY NEED? HOW CAN I GIVE THIS TO MYSELF?

As you begin to practice eating when you're hungry, eating what you want, and stopping when you're full, you become more aware of when you are overeating or undereating for emotional reasons. This is the time to start exploring what is happening on a feeling level for you when you find yourself over- or undereating. You practice asking yourself, "What am I feeling?" and you explore your feelings. You then practice asking yourself, "What do I really need?" and, "How can I give this to myself?" You practice reparenting yourself. Remember, this is just *practicing*. As with practicing any new skill it may seem impossible at first but with each time it gets a little bit easier.

RECLAIMING THE SPIRITUAL SELF

Although this part of the process will probably continue throughout the rest of the mountain and the rest of your life, this is where you begin to explore who you are as a spiritual being. By healing your spiritual wounds, freeing your own creativity, and listening to your spiritual calling, you will nurture the part of your soul that has been buried beneath the obsession with food and weight. As you work on expanding your faith you will find that it will help carry you through the frustrating, overwhelming, and hopeless times ahead.

GOOD CARETAKING, TAKING CARE OF SELF, AND LISTENING TO THE VOICE WITHIN

Feeling your feelings, eating *when* you want, *what* you want, and *how much* you want is the supreme example of good caretaking. Each time you match your feelings with the appropriate response that your soul needs, you are taking care of yourself. Each time you feed yourself as you would feed your child or your best friend, you are taking care of yourself. Each time you pay attention to yourself and listen to the voice within, you are taking care of yourself.

EXPANDING SELF-LOVE AND TRUST

As you go within to understand your various wants, desires, and needs, without judgment or blame, and then start to answer your own call, you fall in love with yourself. You are learning to accept your body exactly as it is, letting go of any expectations to change it. After years of self-hatred, disgust, body loathing, and deprivation it will take some time to trust yourself. However, if you keep loving yourself and listening and answering with compassion and patience, you will become your own best friend.

EMERGENCE OF EMOTIONAL ISSUES

As you start to put your eating, your food, and your weight in the proper perspective, all the feelings that you have been overeating or undereating over, come up and out. These are the feelings you have numbed with food. These are the emotions you have pushed down with obsessional thinking. This is what has been hidden from you for all those years. *But remember, they have always been there!* It is an illusion to think that the food has made them go away. You have dealt with them however you could. Now with the awareness you have developed you have better tools to cope with them.

ANGER, SADNESS, LONELINESS, GRIEF, INNER-CHILD ISSUES (NEGLECT, ABANDONMENT, REJECTION, PHYSICAL OR SEXUAL ABUSE)

Many of these feelings and more come rushing in. There may be childhood wounds from long ago that resurface, creating many different feelings that you don't understand. Expect them. Be ready for them. Don't try to get out of them or discount them. No matter how hurt you have been and how scared you are about feeling the hurt, you can breathe through this stage and witness your own pain. You may need a trusted friend, therapist, or a support group to go through these feelings. Let yourself have whatever you need. Do not deny yourself help in any way. You have developed many survival mechanisms, some more helpful than others. Go within and then let the pain out.

FRUSTRATION, HOPELESSNESS, OVERWHELM, AND OVER/UNDEREATING OCCURRING SIMULTANEOUSLY WITH EMOTIONS

This is the top of the mountain. Many times you have all your feelings *and* you are still overeating or starving yourself. To make matters worse, eating the food or controlling the food doesn't numb you anymore. If you're an overeater you know dieting will never work. If you're an undereater you know that controlling your food doesn't help you anymore. You can hardly stand the feelings you're experiencing. You can't stand yourself, your body, or this stupid process. This is the most difficult part of the process, no doubt about it. Frustration and hopelessness are the two most common feelings during this phase.

You have been working so hard to recover and now you may be eating as you haven't been eating since you started. Your thoughts are filled with how fat you are and how out of control you are. You think how easy it would be just to go on one last diet, and yet you know that isn't the answer. No doubt about it, it is overwhelming.

It takes blind faith to go though this phase. As painful as it can be, this is one of the most powerful parts of the whole journey. It will teach you about yourself and lead the way to knowing how to live the rest of your life with peace and self-love. You will eventually eat like a normal person. You will weigh what you were meant to weigh naturally. You will know and speak your own truth. You will truly experience your feelings of joy, laughter, grief, sadness, and life! This is the top of the mountain and although you may go back and forth many times, you are steadily recovering.

RESOLUTION OF EMOTIONAL ISSUES

At this point in the process you are becoming more experienced at feeling your feelings, expressing them, and having some resolution. It is becoming easier to get in touch with what you are feeling, easier to express it to yourself or others, and easier to take care of yourself emotionally. You may or may not still be over- or undereating. But the intensity of needing to binge or starve is usually beginning to lessen as you process the emotional issues.

LETTING GO OF OVER/UNDEREATING

Once you start learning how to process your feelings and take better care of yourself emotionally, then what you have been practicing with the food (eating when hungry, eating what you want, stopping when full) becomes easier because you no longer have to rely on the food to deal with your feelings. We are not saying that at this point your over- or undereating is completely lifted. For some that may be true. But usually it still requires the daily consciousness of checking in with yourself frequently to see if you are hungry, what you're hungry for, or if you're full yet. You might begin to notice that more often than not you are able to identify when you are emotionally hungry versus physically hungry, and either take care of yourself emotionally or allow yourself to eat. You may be much more adept at identifying what your body wants to eat, instead of what you think you "should" eat. Stopping when you are full, which is usually the last of these three steps to fall into place, also becomes easier as your need to over- or undereat fades. However, now and then you may still over- or undereat, which becomes less important because you are more trusting of your process.

MOURNING THE LOSS OF THE FOOD

Like the loss of a loved one, as your obsession with food dies away it can leave behind a feeling of emptiness. After all, food has been your friend, enemy, and lover. It took up a big part of your life. You could project whatever feelings you wanted onto it. It protected you and kept you from uncomfortable situations. It held a lot of meaning, energy, and time. And as with anything that you finally let go of, you usually experience a loss. Some women in our groups are sad that food no longer serves the purpose it used to. Some feel bittersweet, with a deep gratitude for how the food kept them alive and coping for so long. Some feel scared because now there is a huge hole that exists in their lives. It is different for everyone. Just notice your feelings and if you are experiencing feelings of loss allow yourself to be with them.

REDUCTION IN OBSESSIVE THINKING ABOUT FOOD AND WEIGHT

At this point you are learning to observe your thinking, and if you find yourself obsessing about food, weight, or your body you have the tools to bring your awareness back to your feelings and ask yourself what is going on. Because you are learning to stop the obsessive thinking, be more present in your body, and process your feelings, the obsessive thinking that was once such a big part of your life begins to decrease. We are not saying that it completely disappears . . . it may never completely disappear. But the thoughts become less frequent and intrusive. And when they do pop up you have the tools to stop them and come back to yourself.

A TRANSFORMED RELATIONSHIP TO FOOD AND YOUR BODY

Eventually your relationship to food and your body is transformed. No longer is food your enemy or your lover. No longer do you have to struggle with it or control it. No longer do you feel that it controls you. When you walk into a room full of food you don't have to feel nervous or afraid. You don't even have to remind yourself to watch what you eat. Food has no emotional charge anymore. Eating becomes a natural physical pleasure. This new relationship with food can feel very strange. When you are standing by the dessert table and everyone is talking about how they shouldn't be eating what they are eating it becomes difficult to relate to their obsessing. You might even feel awkward and speechless, not knowing how to describe your experience without either feeling absurd or feeling that you have to go into a lengthy dissertation on your recovery.

The same is true with your body. It is no longer an object for you to project your feelings onto, or to shape, dissect, and torture. You begin to have a deep love and respect for it and can no longer tolerate yourself or anyone else treating it as less than sacred. Again, it can feel strange when you are in the company of other people who are talking about wanting to have a certain body type. It can feel as if you are from another planet. You might even question your own sanity! But eventually your new relationship with food and your body will become more comfortable. With time you will find the language to express what you want. Remember, you have just been through a huge transformation that goes against all of the cultural lessons you have been taught.

OVER/UNDEREATING BECOMES A SIGNAL FOR HELP

At this stage, your over- or undereating and obsessing about food and your body have become powerful tools for you. Now when you begin to overeat, undereat, or obsess, you are conscious of it and you can immediately see your behavior. When you find yourself doing these things they become red flags for you; you know it's time to explore the root cause of these behaviors. You have now developed the tools to look within and find out what feelings are triggering the behavior. You also now have the ability to process the feelings and take care of yourself in whatever way you need to. Even though you may still over- or undereat or obsess now and then, it doesn't happen as often and it shouldn't worry you because you know that you have the tools to turn things around. You are also more trusting of yourself and this process: you know that this happens now and then and it's okay. You actually might even become grateful for having this wonderful signal that lets you know when it's time to pay attention to your Self.

CONTINUED EMOTIONAL PROCESSING

Emotional processing continues for the rest of your life. As new challenges arise in your life, you are now usually able to meet them without relying on food. And if you are not, then you know where to go for help. For some people, many childhood issues have already surfaced and been addressed during the Emergence of Emotional Issues stage, so now the emotional challenges they face stem from more current issues. For other people, however, now that the food and weight are no longer the main focus, they find that their childhood issues are just beginning to surface. It is different for everyone.

The good news is that once you've made it to this place on the mountain you have learned how to be with yourself in a loving, nurturing way. And even though you still go through the normal ups and downs of life, you don't have to abandon yourself anymore. And that is the greatest gift of all.

ACCEPTANCE AND TRUST AND LOVE IN YOURSELF

The acceptance that you have learned for your body and yourself is now part of you, and it transfers to all areas of your life. You now learn to trust yourself in everything you do. And you become very aware of when you are not treating yourself in a loving way, and are able to bring yourself back to being more loving with yourself.

FREEDOM

Freedom from the diet/binge cycle! Freedom from obsessing about food and body! Freedom from being unable to meet your own needs. Freedom from being chained to shoulds and ideals that you can never obtain. Freedom from your own internal repression. Freedom to make your own choices about your food, your body, your needs, and your life! Freedom to listen to your soul's desire and freedom to express who you are in this world. Freedom to be yourself. Freedom to be.

REACHING YOUR NATURAL WEIGHT

At some point in this process you will reach your natural weight. If you eat when you're hungry, eat what your body is hungry for, and stop when you are full, your body will find the size and shape that is genetically natural for you. Keep in mind that many women are already at their natural weight and won't experience any weight loss or gain. *When* you reach this stage is different for everyone. We put it at the end of the mountain map because we want to emphasize that you can have all of the benefits of moving beyond hunger even if you are not yet your natural weight. So many women in our groups start out believing that they can't have a life until they lose a certain number of pounds. And we have seen this disproven over and over again. In fact, you may get so involved in your life that you don't even think about what your weight is anymore. But however it is for you, just trust it.

As you reach your natural weight, you may find that new challenges arise. You may have to learn how to respond to people's comments about your weight loss or gain, and you may have to learn to deal with new issues that your weight was protecting you from (new job, new relationships, and so on). But whatever the challenge, you now have the tools to take care of yourself emotionally. You are ready to live your life.

THE SPIRAL

Failure is impossible.

—Susan B. Anthony

The spiral is another image that we have found helpful in our groups. Many times in the recovery process you may feel as though you are back at square one even though you are making progress. Because there are so many layers of learning, many times newer lessons will trigger old behaviors. For example, one of the first exercises is to eat when you are physically hungry. For individuals with eating disorders, this is a huge challenge. In the very beginning you may begin to feel you are making progress when you start to be able to distinguish between emotional hunger and physical hunger. You find you are increasingly able to eat out of physical hunger rather than emotional hunger. Then as your emotional issues become more conscious, the need to eat compulsively out of emotional hunger becomes more intense. At this point it is not unusual to feel that you have failed. Like a diet, you believe you have fallen off the wagon. But what is actually happening is that you have stepped up to another level of challenge. You now have to learn to process your feelings and, at the same time, eat out of physical hunger. Though it may seem that you are back at square one, or at the same starting point in the circle, you have actually moved up another level. This spiral of progress continues until toward the end of recovery, when instead of automatically eating out of emotional hunger, you have the craving to eat and then can identify that there is an emotional issue that needs to be addressed. Once you begin this recovery process, it is impossible to go back to square one, because the level of consciousness you've now achieved will never go away. You can only travel the spiral in one direction.

Whenever you feel that you have failed, or are not making any progress, or have slid back to the beginning, remember the upward spiral. Draw one to remind yourself of all the growing you have done since you began this process. And remember, we are not saying it is good or bad to be at any certain point on the spiral. You are in the process of unfolding, and like the lotus flower, the unfolding bud is as important as the fully open blossom.

WHEREVER YOU GO, THERE YOU ARE

Everyone's process is different and must only be seen in the context of that person's individual makeup. Many women want to compare themselves to each other in order to determine whether or not they are "right" and "on track." Wherever you are in your own process is where you are supposed to be. Many of you may have other milestones unique to your own recovery that we have not even thought about or acknowledged.

Each different eating disorder also has its own unique recovery process. The bulimic process looks much different from the compulsive eater who does not purge. The woman who weighs far more than her natural weight, and has been ostracized by society is very different from the anorexic. The woman who has gained and lost the same twenty pounds over and over again, and whose life is run by the latest diet fad, has different issues from the woman who has been "overweight" most of her life and has never tried to control her eating. The anorexic who has starved herself to the point of being hospitalized has a very different experience with food from the woman who went on a medically supervised fast in order to lose two hundred pounds.

Many individuals with eating disorders share a bit of all three of the disorders—anorexia, bulimia, and compulsive eating. So the woman in recovery may really feel as if she is going crazy as she goes back and forth, around and around all the stages. Remember, each disorder manifests itself differently and also gets worked out differently. As we describe each of the following disorders, please be aware that they are very simplistic, over-generalized descriptions. Not every anorexic's main issue is control. Not every bulimic is purging their feelings. Not every compulsive eater's body has been physically violated. And, not every woman who is judged as "overweight" by society's standards is overweight and has an eating disorder. The fact is that each individual with an eating disorder has her own unique and complex psychology behind their eating disorder.

When I first started to let myself practice eating when I was hungry and stopping when I was full, I felt that I had tapped into a pain that I wasn't going to be able to bear. For so long I had tried everything I knew to not *listen to my body ! So just asking myself if I was hungry, and then feeling the hunger, was too much. I had been able to diet down to under eighty pounds and kept my weight at that number by not listening to anything my body had to tell me. I* never *tuned in to hunger. I only let myself eat sometimes because I had to. I* never *knew what food my body might want, I only ate what had the least amount of fat or calories. The only feeling I did feel was fullness. But it was a false fullness. I had convinced myself that I could exist on less than five hundred calories a day and be full and satisfied with that. So any amount of food over that felt like way too much. Little by little, I had to learn how to accept normal body feelings. And I am still trying to learn how to let myself weigh what a normal woman of five feet ten should weigh. I know that it is not eighty pounds. For me, this is the hardest part of the whole thing.*

—Tina

Tina, who is anorexic, feels more secure when she is extremely thin and in control. She will feel completely out of control many, many times as she goes through this process. The stage where she is trying to legalize food and let go of control is very hard. Listening to her body as she tries to figure out when she is hungry and when she is full is especially terrifying. To let herself eat whatever her body tells her to, without worrying about fat grams or calories, is one of the hardest instructions to follow. Also, to let her body gain weight in order to go *up* to her natural weight is an exercise in pure faith. Many anorexics' relationship with food is filled with hate and fear. They may relate to their own bodies and selves with distaste, distrust, and loathing. When an anorexic woman can make *total* peace with food, with her body, and with her self, she can fully recover. Somewhere back in her personal history was a very good reason why the anorexic needed to turn to the drastic measures of near starvation. Her challenge now is to learn how to reparent herself in loving and generous ways. She needs to let go and trust in herself to be able to live life on life's terms. A helpful image for some women with these particular issues is to imagine that they are floating peacefully downstream in the river of life. They are the captain of their own ship and are able to look ahead and navigate the many twists and turns of the river. There is no need to hold on to the sticks in the water or grab on to the shore. They can relax, let their own inner spirit guide them and know that they always have a choice.

> *After years and years of eating large amounts of food and then taking laxatives or throwing up as soon as possible, I had no clue how to tune in to what normal hunger or normal fullness felt like. At the end of my eating disorder, I had thrown up after each meal for so long that any amount of food felt like too much. I had to learn how to "sit with" food and fullness. Then, as I was learning how to keep food down, my feelings started to come up. So I had to learn how to "sit with" my feelings and not throw them up either. The other part of the recovery that was particularly hard for me was to let myself eat normally. To my mind, a "normal" portion looked like "not enough," but to my body a "normal" portion felt like too much. I became an observer of how other people ate and asked my friends how they knew what to eat, when to eat, and when to stop. Then I just did what they did until I found my own way.*
>
> —*Abigail*

Abigail's story illustrates how difficult it is for someone whose way of keeping herself safe is to get rid of food or feelings as soon as possible. Often, the bulimic binges when she is overwhelmed by feelings she cannot control and then purges in order to gain back that control. For her to give up control is very scary. She doesn't know what she will do if she has to keep all that food down. She's afraid she will burst, burst with food and burst with feelings. For her, the main part of her recovery is to learn to calm herself down and go through difficult feelings without trying to get away from them. She also has to learn how to have a normal relationship with food. Her relationship with food has been one of distortion. She has eaten much more than what would be considered normal at one sitting. In order to discover what is normal for her, she needs to let herself eat, and then to experience what that amount of food feels like in her body, *without getting rid of it.* At first she might only be able to sit for a few minutes with her fullness before she has to purge. But as she continues trying she can slowly learn to tolerate the feeling of fullness for longer periods of time until she doesn't have to purge at all. It takes practice and trial and error, but most of all it takes perseverance.

By the time I came into this recovery, I was way over three hundred pounds. The shame and guilt of that weight was enormous. Learning why I had needed to put on that much weight helped me to understand myself and start the forgiveness process. However, it did not help me to lose the weight that was on my body. I knew that my weight was a protection for me. I had been molested as a child, molested as a teenager, and molested as an adult. All of those times I was thin. All of those times I thought that I had no right to say no. I had put massive amounts of weight on in order to hide my beauty, my sexual self, my femininity, and my true face. And it worked! No one tried to get close to me. No man tried to molest me. I was safe deep within myself. But I was very unhappy. I longed for an intimate relationship. For children. For a normal life. Keeping the weight on and letting the weight go were equally terrifying to me. I had to learn how to trust myself that when I got to my natural weight I would then be able to say no with my voice and not with my body. It has been a long and hard process. But with each step of the way, as I lost more and more weight, I found the courage and strength to know my boundaries and to be able to hold them.

—Jennifer

Jennifer's struggle with all of the nuances of weight loss is very common. If you are a compulsive eater, and there is an emotional reason for your weight, diets don't work. Until we understand the reason for the weight, work it out, and let it go, we will always just put the weight back on. In recovery, Jennifer learned how to find her own voice and to set boundaries. She went within and healed the childhood wounds of sexual molestation that had kept her a prisoner within her own body for so many years. She learned how to honor and trust her own sexuality and femininity. She learned how to protect herself from harm. She started to believe in herself in ways she had never believed before. She owned and trusted her own power. By the time most of the weight had come off she was clear about who she was and what she wanted. One of the ways she did this was that she learned how to sit with herself and acknowledge her fear of being thin each step of the way. She did not *try* to lose weight. She listened to her body and ate what and how much it wanted. She answered her own call for food, for comfort, and for assurance. She stopped believing that she was "bad" when she was fat and would be "good" when she was thin. She worked on loving herself no matter what her weight. She opened up her heart to herself and to others.

Moving Beyond Hunger

Get out a pencil and piece of paper and draw your own mountain. If you'd like you can use our mountain as a guideline but remember it's just a guideline and feel free to change any parts of it that don't fit for you. You can also just keep your mountain blank and record on it your own stages of recovery as you witness them. On a daily basis, write down somewhere on your mountain a positive statement of where you are in your own process at each step of the way. By positive, we do not mean that positive is "good" and negative is "bad." Some people will be full of anger, fear, rebellion, and overwhelm, and that can be very positive. We mean that you find one piece of your process that is important to your recovery, no matter how small, and that you give yourself credit for being on the path, even if the statement is "I survived today!"

WHEN YOU TRUST your own process you stop the struggle of self-doubt and fear, and can see clearly into your own behaviors and process. To witness respectfully every step you take along the path gives you the insight you need to help you recover. To own your process and see that every part of the recovery, no matter how uncomfortable it may be, is totally necessary, is a positive realization. To tell the truth to yourself, even when the truth does not make you feel any better, is a positive act. To let yourself go up and down the mountain, around and around the spiral, is to set yourself free, free to be who you are, to eat what you want, to weigh what feels best to you, and to live your life with all your feelings.

Chapter 9

RECEIVING THE GIFTS

Our deepest fear is not that we are inadequate. Our deepest fear is that we are powerful beyond measure. It is our light, not our darkness, that most frightens us. We ask ourselves, who am I to be brilliant, gorgeous, talented, and fabulous? Actually, who are you not *to be? You are a child of God. Your playing small doesn't serve the world. There's nothing enlightened about shrinking so that other people won't feel insecure around you. We were born to make manifest the glory of God that is within us. It's not just in some of us; it's in everyone. And as we let our own light shine, we unconsciously give other people permission to do the same. As we are liberated from our own fear, our presence automatically liberates others.*

—Marianne Williamson, *A Return to Love*

Receiving the gifts means embracing our own light within us. It means accepting our eating disorder as a precious gift to us, one that can truly guide us and reveal our life purpose. It is the pearl hidden inside the oyster, causing us irritation until we pry ourselves open and discover the beauty and wisdom that lies within. To find the pearl, it's necessary to open our hearts to our eating disorder and receive it, letting it teach us; it is born from a very wise part of us, one that is fighting to be acknowledged, heard, and given a voice. It's the part within our hearts that wants us to live with fullness, not cut off from our beauty and creativity but free to express who we really are. At times it may feel like a horrible thing that we have to endure and fight and try to control. But that's only because we've stepped into our fear and don't know how to listen and learn from it.

When we try to control our eating disorder by just managing our behavior, we never get to listen to the valuable message that lies hidden in our pain. When we try to fight the disorder then all our energy goes into struggling with it and the symptoms just keep coming back even stronger. Moreover, that energy is energy we could be putting into the manifestation of our greatest dreams and aspirations. When we try to kill the problem by taking pills, purging, or getting operations we just hide the symptoms, we don't even get close to the part of us that is dying to be seen, that must be seen if we're truly to heal and fully realize our hidden potential.

Unfortunately our culture is oriented toward the quick fix, and we are taught to deal only with the symptoms. With eating disorders, our personal growth requires us to go beneath the symptoms and embrace our disorder with open arms and find its message to us.

When we do this, when we open our hearts to our eating disorder and let it teach us, we receive not just one but an abundance of gifts. They come in different forms and at different times. But they do come—in ways we never could have dreamed.

THE COSMIC JOURNEY

By going within to the very depths of your soul, meeting with and then befriending your own personal demons, you will have a better chance to work *with* yourself than *against* yourself. The myth of Persephone is a way to understand how to do just that. The most common version of Persephone is believed by some to be a story that was told after the patriarchal order had taken hold in the world. It shows the sexual violence toward young girls, the inability of their mothers to protect them, and the social realities of many women's lives under male domination. It is centuries old and yet, if not taken literally, describes the rape and objectification of women today. In what very well may be the original story, prior to a patriarchal society, a much more powerful myth of Persephone is told:

As Persephone, the virgin goddess (daughter of the earth mother, Demeter), is out frolicking in the meadow, she hears cries coming up through the cracks in the earth. She stops and puts her ear to the ground. She listens to the cries, moans, and despair of the unhappy dead, the lost voices and pieces of humankind, the parts of people banished into the shadows. Even though she is scared by what she hears, she decides that she cannot ignore these shadowy souls and forgotten spirits. She voluntarily goes down to them, giving them comfort, understanding, compassion, and love.

Her mother, Demeter, is frantic with worry. She doesn't know or understand that her daughter is doing what she must do in order to mature. Even when Persephone is summoned by her grieving mother and the entire world outside, she still chooses to stay and help.

Her mother begs her to come home, to straighten up and not be so "dark" all the time. But in some ways Persephone is happy in the underworld. She has another family in the dark. She learns much about herself and the ways of the world in this place and she wants to stay.

Finally, after a long time, she realizes that she is ready to go back out to the world. She has done all the work she needs to do for now, even though she knows that she will need to return whenever she hears the cries. So, instead of leaving the underworld forever, Persephone agrees to spend part of her life in the underworld and part of it on the earth. She makes a decision to rejoin her mother for only half of the year. She chooses to stay the other half of the year with these inner voices of the underworld no matter how upsetting they might be. She embraces the shadowy world that her mother fears, and incorporates it into her life. She lets herself be completely present with all of the so-called negative voices (the inner world) as well as the so-called positive voices (the outside world). She finds peace and self-knowledge by fully accepting both worlds.

—Laurelee

This myth is a cosmic journey. Our heroine goes to the underworld an immature girl and emerges a mature woman. This story explains the willingness required to listen to the dark realities and inner voices that have been pushed down and buried inside us. To others, who don't understand the process and its rewards, it may look as if we descend into madness when we look into the "other reality" of our wounds, frustrations, and anger. Through this process we may even question our own sanity. We might appear to get a whole lot worse before we get better. And even when we do get better, we are not as we were before. We may not only want to pick flowers and frolic, we may also want to cry or be sad.

However, to stay with your own feelings whatever they may be is the gift that you give to yourself. To have compassion, to answer your own call with love and patience, is what this recovery is about. Each one of you has made the decision to descend into your own personal underworld and find the missing pieces of yourself. Once that decision is made, you will unveil the entire spectrum of your very human feelings. Joy and laughter, sadness and tears become yours to honor, experience, and embrace.

MIRACLES DO HAPPEN

When you dance, the whole universe dances.

—Rumi

Many years ago I did not think that I could have gotten through the day without bingeing or throwing up. Or, when I was in my anorexic phase, I didn't think I could do anything else but starve myself. Then other times I would eat and eat, without purging or excessive exercise to get rid of the food, putting on more and more weight until I couldn't move off the couch. I jumped back and forth through all of the different eating disorders, each time becoming more and more sure that I would be like that forever. I had no idea that someday I would find a way to not only be healed of these terminal diseases, but would actually be grateful for each of them. As I learned to look within for the answers from my soul, I found and heard the voice of my body and my mind. My gratitude to myself for rising above the sure death that I was headed toward is only equaled by the gratitude I have for what I have learned.

In my wildest dreams, I never thought that I could recover. I felt that I was doomed to a life of deprivation and despair. I was isolated and full of shame. I had buried the parts of me that were vulnerable and in so doing I had buried myself alive. I had hidden my light so deep that I only lived in darkness. I did not think that I could continue any longer and I knew something needed to die.

To tell the truth I didn't care if I died. I only wanted to get out of the life that I was living. I had recovered before from a terminal illness when I addressed my alcoholism. Because of that experience, I knew that I needed to do what I was terrified of doing. I needed to trust in something bigger than me. Love was much bigger than me. I let myself surrender to what my disorders were trying to teach me. I started to let go of control and self-hatred. I had tried everything I could think of, but I had never tried that. The greatest gift that I received was getting back my life. I have been blessed with people in my life that have helped me each step of the way. And in return I have been honored to witness others' recoveries.

To say that I am healed of the eating disorders that nearly killed me is a very powerful statement. But even more powerful is the statement of gratitude I give. I will be forever grateful for the risk I took to let go, and the overwhelming support of the universe that I received when I took that chance.

Being willing to embrace the adventure of recovery took courage. Living in fear and self-hatred was something I no longer could do—but it was familiar. To surrender to the unknown is letting go of the familiar and therefore letting go of the walls that protected me for so long. What made it worse was that there weren't many models of true "food and weight" recoveries. However, I drew to me the people and books that would keep me centered on my path. I had to keep an open mind and let information that was new come in. Love, acceptance, understanding, and compassion were all truly new. Little by little I accepted the help of the loving parent within me. I allowed the wisdom of my body to tell me what it needed and the spirit of my soul to guide me. The true miracle of life has graced my entire existence.

—Laurelee

We have done this work for many years and we have been writing this book for many years, too. The beauty of the human spirit has never ceased to amaze us. We have witnessed our own and each other's recoveries, and these continue to unfold. We have been honored to witness the recoveries of many strong and brave women. This alone has made the trip worth it. We know that when you are in the depths of an eating disorder it is very hard to believe that you will ever get out of it. But you will. There is a cure and it is right inside each and every one of us. Just as it was inside both of us, it is inside you. As a great master once said, "Seek and ye shall find." Open yourselves and embrace the mystery of life beyond hunger.

Writing this book is one of the scariest things I've ever done. It means taking who I am and putting it on paper for all to see. It means taking my secret of having an eating disorder, which I held on to tightly for many years, and telling it to the world. I have been so lost in the cycle of bingeing and purging that I couldn't see my way out. I have been full of self-hatred and disappointment for my "failure" to control myself and be thin. I have cringed with shame inside whenever I heard anyone talking about eating disorders. I have witnessed over and over again women's bodies being treated like objects to be manipulated, and I have over and over again done the same to mine. I have been so obsessed with what I shouldn't eat and what I should look like that I completely lost sight of who I truly am. I have dieted for so long and have been educated so well that I forgot how to listen to the wisdom of my body and soul. I have been in the depths of despair, feeling like I was never, ever going to be able to pull myself out.

With time, with loving support, and with patience I have slowly learned to understand the reasons for my eating disorder and to have compassion for myself. I have slowly learned to replace the shame with a deep respect for the way my body and soul fought to reclaim my Self and my truth. To be able to say to the world this is who I am and this is what I've been through is to be able to say to myself that I don't have to hide anymore. I can no longer live without speaking my truth. To do so means going back to overeating, and that is no longer a choice for me. There is no going back.

This is the most precious gift that I have received from this recovery: I get to see and be all of who I am. As I embraced the part of me I had disowned, I reclaimed a huge part of me that I had forgotten: my wisdom, my creativity, and my power. And this is the miracle of transformation. When we are finally able to get a glimpse of who we really are in all of our brilliance, we can't help but fall in love with ourselves.

—Carol

When a miracle presents itself we are always given a choice to embrace and take part in it, or to deny it and step around it. With this book we are inviting you to embrace the miracle and take part in it. We know it is a miracle because when we were in the depths of the bingeing and purging and the never-ending cycle of dieting and self-hatred, we could see no way out. There was no hope—nothing had worked and it felt as though nothing would ever work. It was dark, and the walls around us were very thick and cold. All we could think about then was how we were going to get through the next five minutes without bingeing or throwing up or starving ourselves. Somehow a crack appeared in the wall, and the light filled that crack right up. That's how it works. If you allow just a tiny crack to open, the light will come. And once the foundation of the wall is cracked, eventually the rest has to shatter.

We know that the plan of action we describe in this book isn't the way for everyone. And that doesn't make us or you or anyone else right or wrong. You will know if these ideas are right for you if your soul has been touched by reading this book. Our dream is that, by sharing our own and other women's experiences, you too will be able to embrace the miracle and take part in it. Our prayer is that the miracle will bring you right back into your divine nature . . . because that's where you belong.

Appendix

MOST COMMONLY ASKED QUESTIONS

When will I lose weight?

This is the most frequently asked question. Yet we find that this question is usually more destructive than constructive to the healing process. The answer will be different for everyone. Some people lose weight right away. Others gain weight initially and then return to their natural weight later on. Some learn to love and accept their weight exactly as it is and go on enjoying their life no matter what their weight is. Others, who think that they need to lose weight, find that what they really need to do to reach their natural weight is to maintain their current weight or gain weight.

We feel that a more constructive question might be, "How can I let go of my obsession with losing weight, start to live my life, and take care of myself physically, emotionally, and spiritually?" When you let go of the constant worry of losing weight then you make room for the energy needed to learn how to take care of yourself.

How can I eat whatever I want when I have allergies or dietary restrictions?

You can't, at least not without suffering the consequences. However, there are ways you can approach these restrictions without falling into the diet/binge cycle. There are many individuals who can, based on medical advice, change their diet and feel good about it and have no problem. These people are probably not compulsive eaters. Compulsive eaters use food to take care of themselves emotionally, so to go on a restrictive diet is much more difficult. We have worked with many individuals who, even though they know there is a physical risk in eating a certain food, can't stop.

Many times dietary restrictions based on medical necessity can feel like deprivation, even though you know intellectually it is for your own good. To avoid the feeling of deprivation it's important to be able to find food you are able to eat that is satisfying to you. This may take some time and research, and maybe even some cooking classes. But it is important. The feeling of deprivation is a common trigger for bingeing.

Sometimes having a physician or nutritionist tell you that you can't eat a certain food makes you want to rebel. To avoid this, learn how to make this choice for yourself. Don't avoid these foods just *because you are told to. Avoid these foods because they don't work in your body and won't make you feel well. If you find yourself eating a food that you know is harmful to you—for example, sugar for a diabetic—then ask yourself why you are wanting to hurt yourself, or feel the way that this food makes you feel? Why do you want to feel badly? Is it easier to feel the pain physically than to feel it emotionally?*

It's important to explore the emotional reasons why you are continuing to eat a food even if it hurts your body. It might be difficult to stop hurting yourself until you learn how to take care of yourself emotionally without using food.

I'm a mother of three and I'm always eating standing up or on the run. How can I figure out when I'm hungry or what I'm hungry for when I never have any time or space to do this?

By taking very little steps. Unfortunately there are a variety of situations in our lives that restrict our ability to give ourselves the time and attention that we really need. Mothering is definitely one of these. It is difficult to have the space needed to focus on ourselves when we're trying to attend to thousands of other demands all day long. Sometimes it can feel as if we're housebound and food is the only available way of taking care of ourselves. However, even if you are able to find only fifteen minutes for yourself after the kids are in bed and before you crash from exhaustion, it will help. When you are able to practice listening to your body and your feelings during these fifteen minutes you will find that it becomes easier to do this during the times when you're not alone.

It's very important to be even more patient with yourself in this situation because you don't have the luxury of having time alone for introspection. And with young children at home it may seem like years before you ever will. So give yourself compassion and understanding for what you are doing and allow yourself to take tiny steps.

Every time I try to figure out why I'm eating out of emotional hunger, I come up blank. I can't get in touch with any big feeling. I'm just either bored or stressed. Am I doing something wrong?

No, you are not doing anything wrong. You are actually getting in touch with two very common and very big feelings, boredom and stress. It takes time and practice to learn how to get in touch with the feelings that are linked to the emotional hunger. Sometimes they are layered, meaning that when you first start to explore them you might get a more general feeling (like boredom) and then as you continue to work with this feeling it brings you to another more specific feeling (like loneliness).

Boredom and stress are very important feelings. Boredom suggests that there is some need that isn't being met. If you are bored in the moment, then there is something you are wanting and either can't iden-

tify or don't know how to give it to yourself (see Chapter 6). Stress suggests that there is an emotional feeling that needs to be acknowledged and expressed, that some boundaries in your life need to be set, or that you need to learn how to calm yourself. As you learn to explore your emotions and process them (see Chapter 5), you will be able to pinpoint the core emotional trigger and work with it.

My ankles and knees and back are always killing me and my doctor keeps telling me I need to lose weight. How can I accept my weight when it's causing me physical pain? Besides, I know I'm not myself at this weight.

When we talk about accepting your weight exactly as it is, we are not saying that you have to be at this weight forever. We are saying that in order for you to learn to listen to your bodily needs and meet them, it's important for you to respect your body and love it right where it is, in the moment, because there is a very good reason why it is as it is.

We understand that being overweight can be very painful, physically and emotionally. But it is our experience that hating your body and trying to force it to change, through various forms of deprivation and torture, can be destructive and self-defeating.

It's also important to note that there is new information out dispelling the myth that large people are unhealthy. You can be large and physically fit. There are ways to strengthen your body at whatever weight you are. (See Pat Lyons's and Debby Burgard's book Great Shape *in our Bibliography.)*

Many women say they don't feel like themselves at their current weight. We ask, why? What is it about your weight that doesn't feel like yourself? What is it that is dangerous about being yourself now? Where are you in your body now? What kinds of fantasies do you have about what you'll do or be when you get to be yourself? What do you need to do to take care of yourself so that you can start to be your true self regardless of your weight?

I am sure that if I stop controlling my food I will be completely out of control. I have tried it and I have gone on huge binges that were terrible. What if this works for everyone but me?

The process of allowing yourself to eat whatever you want is, once again, different for everyone. Some people can go out one day, fill their cupboards with all of their forbidden foods, and within a month have no desire to binge on any of them anymore. Others need to start slowly, and let go of control of one food at a time, working with this food until they no longer feel deprived about not having it or feel guilty about eating it. In this way they explore how to take care of themselves emotionally when they are bingeing on this food.

As we've said in Chapter 4, just allowing yourself to eat whatever you want, without working on the underlying emotional issues, might lead to one very long binge. If you are eating emotionally, then you will need to learn how to take care of yourself emotionally before you can put down the food. If you've tried to stop dieting without any success, you might look for additional support to help you explore your emotional eating. That might mean seeing a therapist who can understand the process we describe here or joining a group that is working on similar issues.

I know I need help with my eating disorder but I'm scared to go to a therapist because the last one told me I needed to stop eating fats and start exercising. When I told her I had tried that and it didn't work for me, she told me I was in denial. I tried to do what she asked but I couldn't, so I found myself just lying to her. I finally just didn't go back. Is therapy not for me?

Just because a particular therapist wasn't for you doesn't mean therapy isn't for you. Every therapist has a different approach, which works for some people and not for others. It's important for you to be able to find a therapist who meets your needs. As women, we're not taught to be assertive about meeting our needs, so to go and interview a number of therapists and select one can seem overwhelming. But it is very important to find a therapist that you can trust and feel safe with and who has an approach that you want. Unfortunately, you may not know what you want until you find out what it is you don't want.

Most types of therapy have a county, state, or national organization that can offer tips on how to find a therapist. But if you've had one bad experience, don't give up. There are as many different approaches to treating eating disorders as there are therapists.

I tried to stop dieting two years ago. But it seems like every six months I get fed up with my weight and I go on another diet. I feel good for a few weeks and then before I know it I'm bingeing again. I know diets don't work, but why do I keep doing them?

It takes an incredible amount of courage not to diet in this society, especially if you sometimes lose weight on them. It's very hard to stop believing that this time, with this diet, it will be different and the weight won't ever be put back on, even when you have proved over and over to yourself that this statement is untrue! Diets are very appealing. You can change something you do not like about yourself in a very short period of time. The problem is that for most people, diets don't work in the long term. If what you are trying to do is feed yourself emotionally, then diets will never help you do that. What starts to happen if you take away your method of coping without working on the underlying feelings as they come up is that the need to eat becomes stronger than your desire to be thinner. And another diet hits the dust and you start eating and eating. Then as you begin to feel more and more out of control about your food and your weight, the next thing you know you are back to thinking about another diet in order to gain control of yourself again. This can be repeated as often as you can stand it. Learn to recognize overeating as a "red flag." Then learn how to listen, and eventually there will not be any reason for you to continue to overeat. Working with yourself like this enables you to let go of dieting and the seduction of fast weight loss.

There are certain foods I know that if I just eat one bite, I will go on a month-long binge. How can you say we should give ourselves permission to eat everything?

If you have judged some foods to be "bad" or "addictive" or "taboo," then unless you have worked to really legalize them and make them "neutral," you will forever bump up against the charge around those certain foods. Many times we want what we think we cannot have. So depriving yourself of certain foods that you like will only make you want to binge on those foods later. However, compulsive eaters eat for many different reasons, deprivation is only one of them. So if you have decided that the only reason you binge is because a certain food is "bad" "addictive," or "taboo," many important insights to your own behavior are ignored. The best thing to do is to let yourself feel abundant about all foods and then from within *your body let yourself choose what is right for you.*

I have been bulimic for two years and I desperately want to stop purging. I realize that I have to be willing to let myself eat without worrying how I can get rid of it, but if I binge, I can't stand to have the food left in my stomach. How do I stop throwing up?

Most people who discover purging as a way to eat a lot of food without the weight gain to go with it start out using bulimia as a "diet aid." Giving up dieting and all forms of control about food means letting yourself "sit" with the food that you have eaten. This takes time and patience and is part of the process that cannot be rushed. Becoming conscious means letting yourself know what you are really doing by bingeing and purging. When a person binges and then purges it's almost as if the binge never happened. Then letting go of the judgment about your behavior is what will give you the strength to start to understand what you can do instead. All forms of bulimia, binge eating and then vomiting, excessive exercising, using diuretics and laxatives, are ways you have found to cope with many different feelings and experiences. When you learn other ways to nurture yourself and are able to implement them, you will be able to let go of the need not only to binge but you will also be able to stop purging those binges away.

I'm sick and tired of everybody looking and worrying about what I'm eating. My parents are always trying to get me to eat. I have to go to my doctor every week and be weighed. My friends are always telling me to eat more. How can I ever do it myself if everyone is doing it for me?

If you have dieted to a point of near starvation, people get worried. Even if you feel that you are recovering from anorexia and are able to take back your right to feed yourself, your friends and family may not be where you are yet. The best thing to do is to be clear that you are on the road to wellness and that your body *will always be able to let you know* when *you are hungry,* what *you are hungry for, and* when *to stop. It will take some time to learn the messages of your body, especially if they have been totally ignored and your weight is 20 percent below your natural body weight. You are building a relationship of trust with yourself and at the same time you may have to build a relationship of trust with the people around you as well. Communicate with them as much as you can that you need their support to learn from* yourself *what your body needs to do. Therapy, group support, and education about eating disorders and the cure for eating disorders is extremely helpful for all. But the most important thing to do is to listen within to your own body.*

I know that I'm eating, I know why I'm eating, but I just can't stop eating. I'm terrified and frustrated and sick of it. What can I do?

We find that many women begin feeling this way when they are at the top of the mountain, one of the most difficult places in this recovery (see Chapter 7). This is where you are becoming aware of your feelings and are able to see what you're eating to repress, but you can't stop eating. We usually say, Congratulations! You've made it to the top of the mountain! It may not feel very good, but it is progress. It means that you are no longer stuffing your feelings down with food—you are having them despite the food. It is a very important place to be in this recovery, and it's a very important place to work through.

The work now is to continue to take care of yourself emotionally so that you learn to trust yourself with your own feelings. You are learn-

ing that there are other ways of coping with your feelings besides using food. It may take time to get to the point where you actually feel secure enough to put down the food. It's also important to continue practicing eating when you're hungry, eating what you're hungry for, and stopping when you're full.

We can't tell you how long this stage of recovery lasts—it is different for everyone. Stay with yourself and know that you are in the most challenging place of the journey. It will end, and you will move on. If it becomes too overwhelming, get support. You don't have to do it alone.

What do I do about exercise? I'm afraid if I go running or go to the gym I will get back into the "diet mentality" and want to work out more in order to lose weight instead of just doing it because it feels good.

Like all other parts of this process the most important thing is to go slow and easy on yourself. Keep in touch with why *you want to work out. If it's for health and the good feeling that you can get by moving your body, then great! If it's because you think that you "should" because it will make you lose weight, look out! The fact that our bodies were designed to move and be fit, strong, and healthy is why many times our bodies crave exercise. So if the signal we get from our bodies is to do yoga, walk, run, bike, dance or any of the ways of movement that makes us feel good, listen to the signal and let yourself go. But if we have judged ourselves and our bodies as bad because they are pudgy, jiggily, weak, or in need of improvement, then it is very easy to use exercise as a whip to punish us into shape. That obviously doesn't work very well. As you start an exercise program be clear and honest with yourself about why you are drawn to it and go from there. If it's for the health of your body, mind, and spirit, then only good will come from it.*

Ever since I started with this way of eating I can't believe how much junk food I eat all the time! I'm so sick of candy, potato chips, ice cream, and chocolate. When can I stop eating like this?

Whenever you want to. A lot of the time the clients who come into Beyond Hunger get mad at us because they think just because they have legalized all food and can eat anything that they want, then that means they should only eat food that has previously been "off limits." They feel that they must eat only "junk" and they are sick of it. It's understandable that if you have been on a diet and deprived of all the foods that are "bad" for you for a long time, when they are first brought into your life all you want to do is eat is those foods. This is part of the process. But eventually you will want a salad or a vegetable, which until this point had been a "diet food." Our bodies crave a lot of different foods. Letting yourself eat what your body wants *is also letting yourself eat foods that you once only ate when you were dieting. It's perfectly okay to eat whatever foods your body wants and it's perfectly okay* not *to eat what it doesn't want. You need to become your own "diet expert" and let your body tell you what foods work best for you.*

Soon after starting this recovery I began to throw up again. This is something I had stopped doing about two years ago, even though I would still binge and then diet. What is happening?

Bingeing and purging are coping mechanisms. When a compulsive eater is under stress, she turns to food. If you've stopped throwing up but are still bingeing and dieting, you have only stopped one of the symptoms (throwing up) but you haven't addressed the core issues that are causing the overeating. As you start to explore these issues and feelings come up that you can't yet cope with, you may regress to old behaviors (such as throwing up). This can also happen to anorexics: when they stop controlling their foods they may start binge eating. This recovery will bring to the surface the things that you binged over. *Remember that you always have a choice. You can eat and then purge to make yourself feel better, or you can stay conscious and go through your feelings as much as possible. As you get better at taking care of yourself emotionally, it will get easier to choose to feel your feelings instead of purging, overeating, or undereating. Another reason that old behaviors may come back is that you may not have really given yourself permission to eat, so you feel very bad and scared when you binge. This is also normal. Bingeing and then purging, exercising excessively, or dieting are all forms of trying to control your food. Just be aware of how you are trying to help yourself through a stressful time or through a time when you are afraid that you will get "too fat" in this recovery.*

The most helpful thing you can do for yourself is to legalize everything you do and just stay connected to yourself. Ask yourself each time you feel the need to binge, purge, diet, or obsess about your body, "What am I feeling right now? What do I really need right now? How can I help myself through this?" Then compassionately, gently, and patiently give yourself what you truly need.

I have tried everything. I have tried every diet, every exercise, I have had my stomach stapled, and I have tried all kinds of medication in pills, liquids, and shots. To try this way feels like the only way left. What if I fail again?

It is not unusual for people to fail at every diet. Diets have a 95 percent failure rate. This is not because you are weak willed or stubborn. It's because diets never have and never will work. Eating when you're hungry, eating what you're body wants, and stopping when you're full is not a diet. It is a way to eat naturally, according to your own body. The way your body eats is as unique as you are yourself. Give yourself over to the wisdom of your body and trust what it tells you to do. You can not go on or off anything. At the same time, learn why you have overeaten for reasons other than hunger in the past and learn from these experiences. Learn ways to nurture yourself other than with food. Find out who you are and what you want. Stay close to yourself and go through this process lovingly and gently. Support your recovery and you will not fail.

BIBLIOGRAPHY

Anderson, Sherry Ruth, and Patricia Hopkins. *The Feminine Face of God: The Unfolding of the Sacred in Women.* New York: Bantam Books, 1991.

Bennett, Hal Zina. *Write from the Heart: Unleashing the Power of Your Creativity.* Novato, CA: Nataraj Publishing, 1995.

Bennett, William, and Joel Gurin. *The Dieter's Dilemma.* New York: Basic Books, 1982.

Bode, Janet. *Food Fight: A Guide to Eating Disorders for Pre-teens and Their Parents.* New York: Simon & Schuster, 1997.

Boorstein, Sylvia. *It's Easier Than You Think: The Buddhist Way to Happiness.* San Francisco: HarperCollins, 1995.

Bordo, Susan. *Unbearable Weight: Feminism, Western Culture and the Body.* Los Angeles: University of California Press, 1993.

Bradshaw, John. *Healing the Shame that Binds You.* Deerfield, FL: Health Communications, 1988.

Brumberg, Joan Jacobs. *Body Project: An Intimate History of American Girls.* New York: Random House, 1997.

Callan, Dawn. *Awakening the Warrior Within: Secrets of Personal Safety and Inner Security.* Novato, CA: Nataraj Publishing, 1995.

Cameron, Julia. *The Artist's Way: A Spiritual Path to Higher Creativity.* New York: Tarcher/Putnam, 1992.

Chernin, Kim. *The Obsession: Reflections on the Tyranny of Slenderness.* New York: Harper & Row, 1981.

Duerk, Judith. *A Circle of Stones: Woman's Journey to Herself.* San Diego: LuraMedia, 1989.

Eisler, Riane. *The Chalice and the Blade: Our History, Our Future.* San Francisco: Harper & Row, 1987.

Estes, Clarissa Pinkola. *Women Who Run with the Wolves: Myths and Stories About the Wild Woman Archetype.* New York: Ballantine, 1992.

Fallon, Patricia, Melanie Katzman, and Susan Wooley. *Feminist Perspectives on Eating Disorders.* New York: The Guilford Press, 1994.

Faludi, Susan. *Backlash: The Undeclared War Against Women.* New York: Crown, 1991.

Foster, Patricia, ed. *Minding the Body: Women Writers on Body and Soul.* New York: Doubleday, 1994.

Fraser, Laura. *Losing It: America's Obsession with Weight and the Industry That Feeds on It.* New York: Random House, 1997.

Gadon, Elinor W. *The Once and Future Goddess: A Symbol for Our Times.* New York: Harper & Row, 1989.

Gaesser, Glenn A. *Big Fat Lies.* New York: Ballantine, 1996.

"Getting Slim." *U.S. News & World Report,* 14 May 1990, pp. 56–65.

Goodman, Charisse W. *The Invisible Woman: Confronting Weight Prejudice in America.* Carlsbad, CA: Gurze Books, 1995.

Hancock, Emily. *The Girl Within.* New York: Fawcett Columbine, 1989.

Hirschmann, Jane R., and Carol H. Munter. *Overcoming Overeating.* Reading, MA: Addison-Wesley, 1988.

———. *When Women Stop Hating Their Bodies: Freeing Yourself from Food and Weight Obsession.* New York: Fawcett Columbine, 1995.

Hirschmann, Jane R., and Lela Zaphiropoulos. *Preventing Childhood Eating Problems: A Practical Positive Approach to Raising Kids Free of Food and Weight Conflicts.* (Originally titled *Are You Hungry?*) Carlsbad, CA: Gurze Books, 1993.

Hsu, L. K. George, M.D. *Eating Disorders.* New York: The Guilford Press, 1990.

Hutchinson, Marcia Germaine. *Transforming Body Image: Learning to Love the Body You Have.* Freedom, CA: The Crossing Press, 1985.

Ikeda, Joanne P. *Am I Fat? Helping Children Accept Differences in Body Size.* Berkeley, CA: ETR Associates, 1992.

Johnson, Karen. *Trusting Ourselves: The Complete Guide to Emotional Well-Being for Women.* New York: Atlantic Press, 1990.

Johnston, Andrea. *Girls Speak Out: Finding Your True Self.* New York: Scholastic Inc, 1996.

Kasl, Charlotte. *Women, Sex, and Addiction: A Search for Love and Power.* New York: Harper & Row, 1989.

Kornfield, Jack. *A Path with Heart.* New York: Bantam Books, 1993.

Leonard, Linda Schierse. *Meeting the Madwoman: An Inner Challenge for Feminine Spirit.* New York: Bantam Books, 1993.

Lerner, Harriet Goldhor. *The Dance of Anger: A Woman's Guide to Changing the Patterns of Intimate Relationships.* New York: Harper & Row, 1986.

———. *The Dance of Intimacy: A Woman's Guide to Courageous Acts of Change in Key Relationships.* New York: Harper & Row, 1989.

———. *The Dance of Deception: A Guide to Authenticity and Truth-telling in Women's Relationships.* New York: HarperCollins, 1993.

Lyons, Pat, and Debby Burgard. *Great Shape: The First Fitness Guide for Large Women.* Palo Alto, CA: Bull Publishing, 1990.

Mellin, L. M., C. E. Irwin, Jr., and S. Scully. "Disordered Eating Characteristics in Girls: A Survey of Middle Class Children." *Journal of the American Dietetic Association* 92 (1992): 851–53.

Orbach, Susie. *Fat Is a Feminist Issue: A Self-Help Guide for Compulsive Eaters.* London: Hamlyn, 1979.

———. *Fat Is a Feminist Issue II: The Anti-Diet Guide to Permanent Weight Loss.* New York: Berkley, 1982.

———. *Hunger Strike: An Anorexic's Struggle as a Metaphor for Our Age.* New York: Norton, 1986.

Orbach, Susie, and Louise Eichenbaum. *Between Women: Love, Envy, and Competition in Women's Friendships.* New York: Viking Penguin, 1988.

Orenstein, Peggy. *Schoolgirls: Young Women, Self-Esteem, and the Confidence Gap.* New York: Anchor Books, 1994.

Pipher, Mary. *Reviving Ophelia: Saving the Selves of Adolescent Girls.* New York: Ballantine, 1994.

Polivy, Janet. "Psychological Consequences of Food Restriction." *Journal of the American Dietetic Association* 96 (1996): 589.

Polster, Miriam F. *Eve's Daughters: The Forbidden Heroism of Women.* San Francisco: Josey-Bass Publishers, 1992.

Radiance: The Magazine for Large Women 510: 482–680. P.O. Box 30246, Oakland, CA 94604.

Reilly, Patricia Lynn. *A God Who Looks Like Me: Discovering a Woman-Affirming Spirituality.* New York: Ballantine, 1995.

Rodin, Judith. *Body Traps: Breaking the Binds That Keep You from Feeling Good About Your Body.* New York: Morrow, 1992.

Roth, Geneen. *Feeding the Hungry Heart: The Experience of Compulsive Eating.* New York: Signet, 1983.

———. *Breaking Free from Compulsive Eating.* New York: Signet, 1986.

———. *Why Weight? A Guide to Ending Compulsive Eating.* New York: Penguin Books, 1989.

———. *When Food Is Love: Exploring the Relationship Between Eating and Intimacy.* New York: Penguin Books, 1991.

Rumney, Avis. *Dying to Please: Anorexia Nervosa and Its Cure.* London: McFarland, 1983.

Schoenfielder, Lisa, and Barb Wieser. *Shadow on a Tightrope: Writings by Women on Fat Oppression.* Iowa City: Aunt Lute Book Company, 1983.

Schweitzer-Mordecai, Ruth. *Spiritual Freedom: Healing Shame-Based Spirituality.* Point Richmond, CA: Dreamsmith Ink, 1996.

Seid, Roberta Pollack. *Never Too Thin: Why Women Are at War with Their Bodies.* New York: Prentice-Hall, 1989.

Spretnak, Charlene, ed. *The Politics of Women's Spirituality: Essays of Founding Mothers of the Movement.* Garden City, NY: Anchor Books, 1982.

Steinem, Gloria. *The Revolution from Within: A Book of Self-Esteem.* Boston: Little, Brown & Co., 1992.

Stone, Merlin. *When God Was a Woman.* New York: Harcourt Brace Jovanovich, 1978.

Stormer, S. M., and J. K. Thompson. "Explanations of Body Image Disturbance: A Test of Maturational Status, Negative Verbal Commentary, Social Comparison, and Sociocultural Hypotheses." *International Journal of Eating Disorders* 19(1996): 193–202.

Thompson, Becky W. *A Hunger So Wide and So Deep: American Women Speak Out on Eating Problems.* Minneapolis/London: University of Minnesota Press, 1995.

Tiggeman M., and A. S. Pickering. "Role of Television in Adolescent Women's Body Dissatisfaction and Drive for Thinness." *International Journal of Eating Disorders* 20(1996): 199–203.

Waterhouse, Debra. *Like Mother, Like Daughter: How Women Are Influenced by Their Mother's Relationship with Food and How to Break the Pattern.* New York: Hyperion, 1997.

Wolfe, Naomi. *The Beauty Myth: How Images of Beauty Are Used Against Women.* New York: William Morrow & Co., 1991.

Women's Therapy Centre Institute. *Eating Problems: A Feminist Psychoanalytic Treatment Model.* New York: Basic Books, 1994.

Woodman, Marion. *The Owl Was a Baker's Daughter: Obesity, Anorexia Nervosa, and the Repressed Feminine—A Psychological Study.* Toronto, Canada: Inner City Books, 1980.

———. *Addicton to Perfection: The Still Unravished Bride.* Toronto, Canada: Inner City Books, 1982.

———. *The Pregnant Virgin: A Process of Psychological Transformation.* Toronto, Canada: Inner City Books, 1985.

Wooley, Wayne, M.D., and Susan Wooley, M.D. "33,000 Women Tell How They Really Feel About Their Bodies." *Glamour,* February 1984.

INDEX

ABOUT BEYOND HUNGER

Beyond Hunger, Inc. is a nonprofit organization that provides support groups, workshops, and education for adults and adolescents struggling with eating disorders, using a nondiet approach that explores the psychological and cultural reasons underlying compulsive eating.

Beyond Hunger's philosophy is that eating disorders are symptoms of deeper cultural and/or psychological issues that need to be addressed to achieve long-term recovery. Beyond Hunger helps its participants to develop compassion and understanding for their eating disorders; explore the underlying feelings related to over- or undereating; identify and respond to physiological cues of hunger, fullness, and satisfaction; create a more positive and loving relationship to the self and the body; and develop alternative ways of nurturing the self.

If you would like to purchase a tape recording of the guided imageries in this book, contact Beyond Hunger at the address below. For more information about Beyond Hunger, or to make a tax-deductible donation, please feel free to call or write us at:

Beyond Hunger, Inc.
P.O. Box 151148
San Rafael, California 94915-1148
(415) 459-2270
BeyondHunger. ORG